White Rose MATHS

Year 1

Maths Practice Journal

Author: Caroline Hamilton

Series Editor: MK Connolly

OXFORD
UNIVERSITY PRESS

Contents

Autumn term
Block 1   Place value

In this block, we **count** using **ten frames**.
This ten frame shows 7

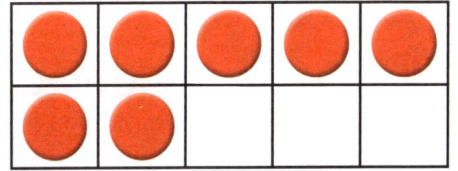

4
8
2

two
four
eight

We write numbers in different ways.
We match up **words** and **numerals**.

4	5	6	

We also complete **number tracks**.
7 comes next on this one.

We use number lines to find **1 more** and **1 less.**
I've circled 1 more than 6 here.

0   1   2   3   4   5   6   ⑦   8   9   10

Here are some maths words that you'll see.
Can you remember what they mean?

more than   less than   smallest   greatest
counting forward/back   how many   1 more/1 less

Place value

Date:

Let's practise

1 Circle the objects to show two sets.

2 How many apples are there?

There are ☐ apples.

3 How many counters are there?

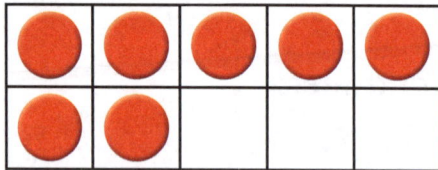

There are ☐ counters.

4 Draw 4 counters.

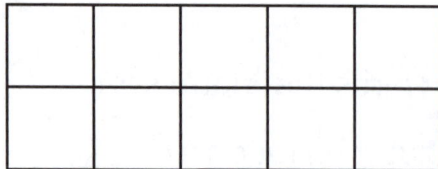

5 How many counters are there?

There are ☐ counters.

6 How many leaves are there?

There are ☐ leaves.

7 Circle 3 pears.

8 Colour 7 triangles.

9 Circle 4 carrots and 6 horses.

10 Draw 6 counters in two different ways.

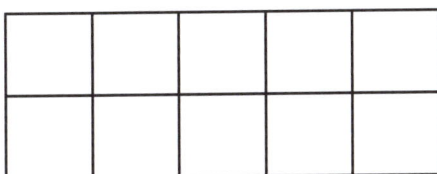

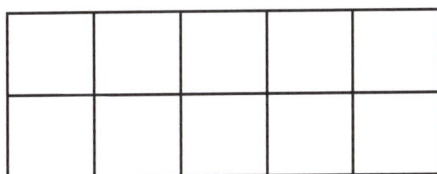

🏠 Real world maths

Get 10 small objects.

Count out 3 of them.

Put them all back together.

Count out 7 of them.

Put them all back together.

Count out 9 of them.

> How many objects are there? Does it matter which object you count first?

💬 Talk it out

How many different ways can you sort the buttons?

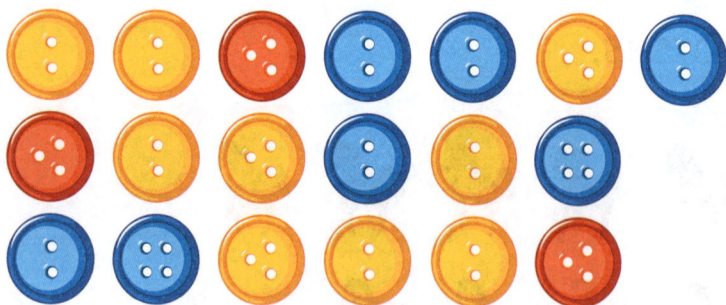

> What is the same about all the objects? What is different?

💬 I can sort the buttons by . . .

💬 I can make . . . sets of . . . buttons.

How did you find these questions?   🙂 😐 🙁

Place value

Let's practise

1   a)   Draw counters to show the apples.

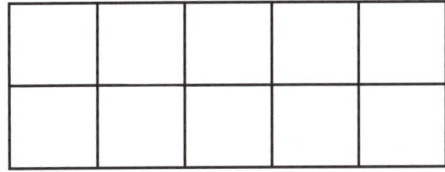

b)   How many apples are there?

There are ☐ apples.

2   a)   Draw counters to show the cookies.

b)   How many cookies are there?

There are ☐ cookies.

3   Draw counters to show each number.
Then write the numeral to match.

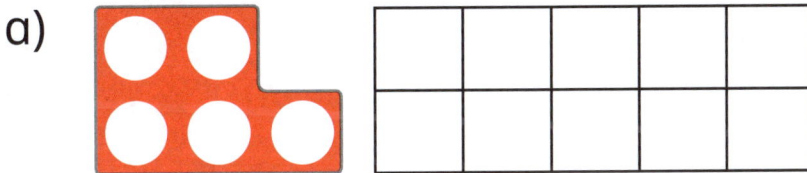

a)

How many
counters do
you need?

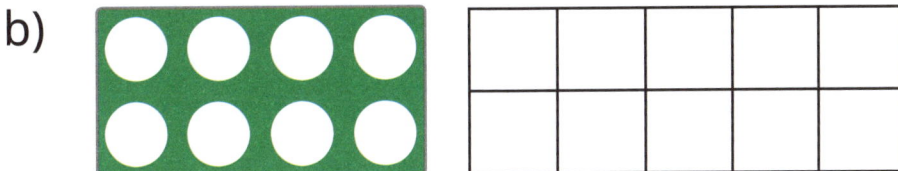

b)

4   Tick the correct word for each numeral.

7	one	seven	zero
3	three	five	four
9	nine	eight	ten
0	one	two	zero
5	four	six	five

A **numeral** is a symbol, like 1 or 4, that stands for a number.

5   a)   Colour 2 circles.

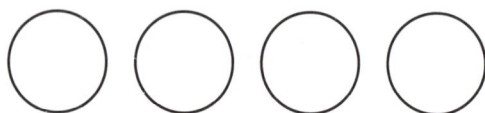

   b)   Colour 6 squares.

6   Complete the number tracks.

   a)

0	1	2	3			

   b)

5	6					

What number are you starting from? What comes next?

7   Max is counting from 5

Five, six, eight, nine, ten ...

Tick the number Max has missed.

four		one		seven

🏠 Real world maths

Draw counters to show how old you are.

How old are you?
So how many counters
do you need?

💬 Talk it out

Count out loud from each number until you reach 10

| 4 | 3 | 6 | 2 | 7 |

💬 I will start at 7
7, 8, 9, 10

💬 I will start at 2 ...

How did you find these questions?   🙂 😐 ☹️

9

Place value

Date:

Let's practise

1 a)   Draw 1 more than 2

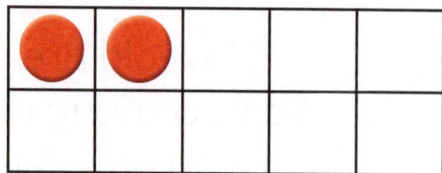

1 more than 2 is ☐

b)   Draw 1 more than 6

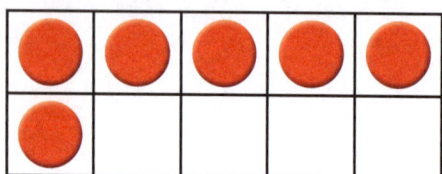

1 more than 6 is ☐

2 Circle 1 more than 9

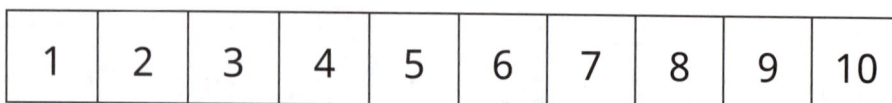

| 1 | 2 | 3 | 4 | 5 | 6 | 7 | 8 | 9 | 10 |

1 more than 9 is ☐

3 Complete the sentences.

a)   1 more than 3 is ☐

b)   1 more than 5 is ☐

4 Tiny is counting back.

What mistake has Tiny made?

4, 2, 1

_____

5 Complete the number tracks.

a)

| 10 | 9 | 8 | 7 | | | | | | |

b)

| 7 | 6 | 5 | | | |

c)

| 8 | | | 5 | 4 | | | |

6 a) Circle 1 less than 3

| 1 | 2 | 3 | 4 | 5 | 6 | 7 | 8 | 9 | 10 |

1 less than 3 is ☐

b) Circle 1 less than 7

| 1 | 2 | 3 | 4 | 5 | 6 | 7 | 8 | 9 | 10 |

1 less than 7 is ☐

7 Complete the sentences.

a) 1 less than 4 is ☐

b) 1 less than 10 is ☐

How can counting help you to find 1 less?

8 Find the missing number.

☐ is 1 less than 8

💭 Think it out

Ron has these number cards: 🔴 🔺 💜

🔴 is 1 less than 🔺

💜 is 1 less than 🔴

💜 is 1 more than 6

What is the value of each card?

🔴 is ☐   🔺 is ☐   💜 is ☐

🏠 Real world maths

Choose one of the activities.

Do 10 star jumps.
Count back from 10 as you jump.

Hop 10 times.
Count back from 10 as you hop.

Clap 10 times.
Count back from 10 as you clap.

Blink 10 times.
Count back from 10 as you blink.

Should you stop counting at 1 or zero?

How did you find these questions?   🙂 😐 🙁

Place value

Date:

Let's practise

1   a)   Can each dog have a bone? _____

b)   Can each child have a cookie? _____

2   Tick the bag that has one apple for each horse.

3   Tick the picture that matches the sentence.

There are fewer triangles than circles.

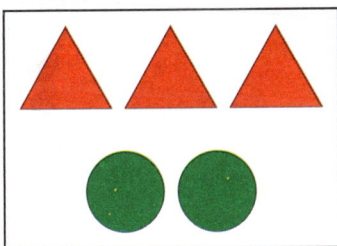

Remember that **fewer** means a smaller amount.

4   a)   Draw fewer than 5 counters.

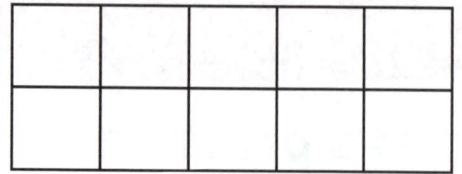

b)   Draw more than 8 counters.

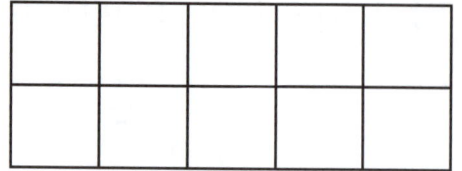

5   Eva has 8 marbles.

Mo has 7 marbles.

Who has fewer marbles? _____

6   Use the words to complete the sentences.

| less than | greater than | equal to |

a)   3 is _____ 6

b)   0 is _____ 2

c)   Four is _____ two.

7   Write <, > or = to compare the numbers.

2 ◯ 1

four ◯ nine

5 ◯ 5

What does each symbol mean?

8   Write a number to make this correct.

☐ < 7

How many different ways can you find?

🏠 Real world maths

Use the words **fewer** and **more** in a sentence each day this week.

Write what you say.

I have 6 more marbles than my brother. He has fewer marbles than me.

_____

_____

_____

_____

💬 Talk it out

Find all the ways to complete the number sentence.

10 > ☐ > 3

How many ways can you find?

How did you find these questions?   🙂 😐 ☹

15

Place value

Date:

Let's practise

1 a) How many animals are in each group?

group 1

group 2

group 3

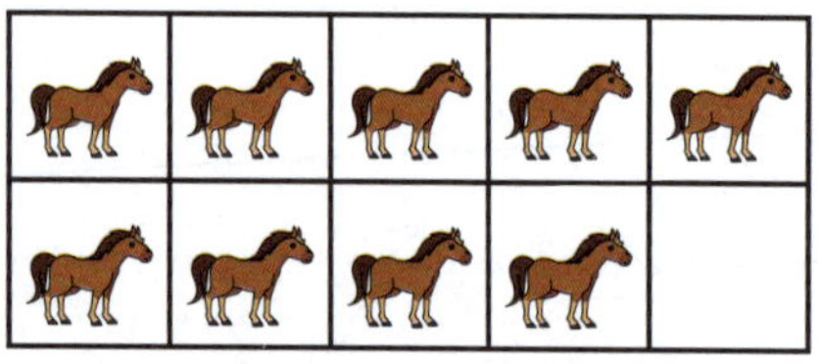

b) The smallest group is group

c) The greatest group is group

d) There are more dogs than _____ .

e) There are _____ sheep than horses.

2 Write the numbers from smallest to greatest.

a) 4, 1, 3   [   ] , [   ] , [   ]

b) 10, 9, 6   [   ] , [   ] , [   ]

c) 0, 5, 4   [   ] , [   ] , [   ]

3 Write the numbers from greatest to smallest.

a) 7, 8, 4 ☐ , ☐ , ☐

b) 3, 6, 10 ☐ , ☐ , ☐

4 Circle the number three.

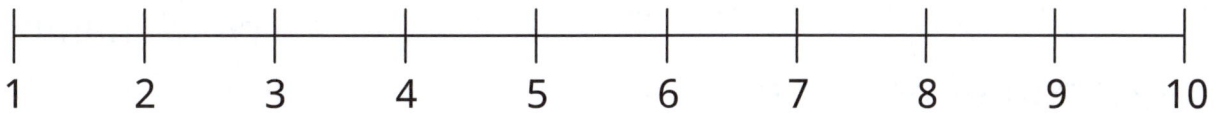

```
├───┼───┼───┼───┼───┼───┼───┼───┼───┤
1   2   3   4   5   6   7   8   9   10
```

5 Circle 1 more than 6

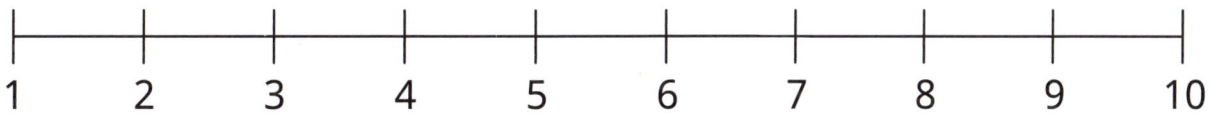

```
├───┼───┼───┼───┼───┼───┼───┼───┼───┤
1   2   3   4   5   6   7   8   9   10
```

6 Here is part of a number line.

Complete the number line.

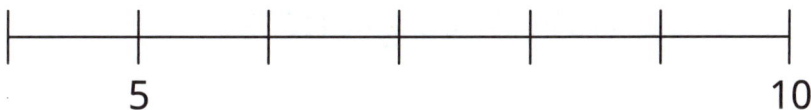

```
├───┼───┼───┼───┼───┼───┤
   5                   10
```

7 What number is the arrow pointing to?

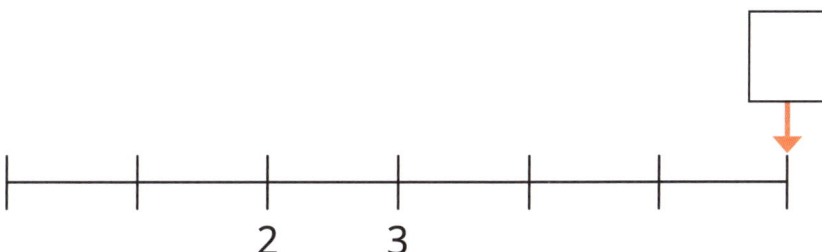

☐

```
├───┼───┼───┼───┼───┤
   2   3
```

🏠 Real world maths

0   **1**   **3**

Using paper and string make your own number line.

Hide some of the numbers.

See if someone at home can guess what you have hidden.

> Which number is missing? How do you know?

💭 Think it out

Roll 3 dice.

Put the dice in order from smallest to greatest.

Roll 3 dice again.

Put the dice in order from greatest to smallest.

> How do you know which is the greatest? How do you know which is the smallest?

How did you find these questions? 🙂 😐 🙁

Autumn term
Block 2 Addition and subtraction

In this block, we look at **parts** and **wholes**.

2 is a part. 3 is a part.

The whole is 5

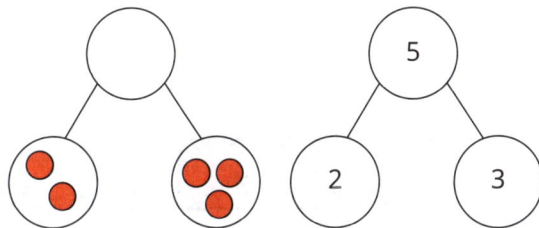

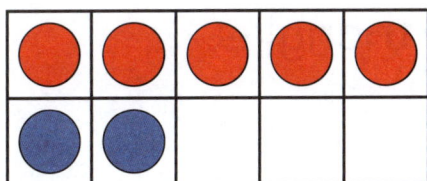

We also **add** numbers using **ten frames**.

This one shows 5 + 2 = 7

We use **number lines** to **subtract** numbers.
This one shows 8 – 5 = 3

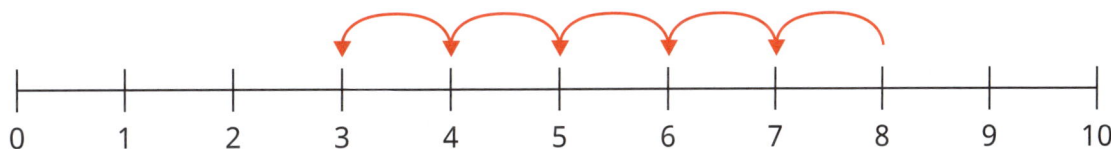

0   1   2   3   4   5   6   7   8   9   10

We also use **bar models** to show parts and wholes.

These help us find **fact families** using **number bonds**.

10	
6	4

6 + 4 = 10   10 = 6 + 4

4 + 6 = 10   10 = 4 + 6

Here are some maths words that you'll see.

Can you remember what they mean?

whole   part   add   subtract   fact family

number bond   how many more   how many left

Addition and subtraction

Date:

Let's practise

1 There are 5 shapes.

a) Complete the sentence.

There are ☐ squares and ☐ triangles.

b) Draw the parts.

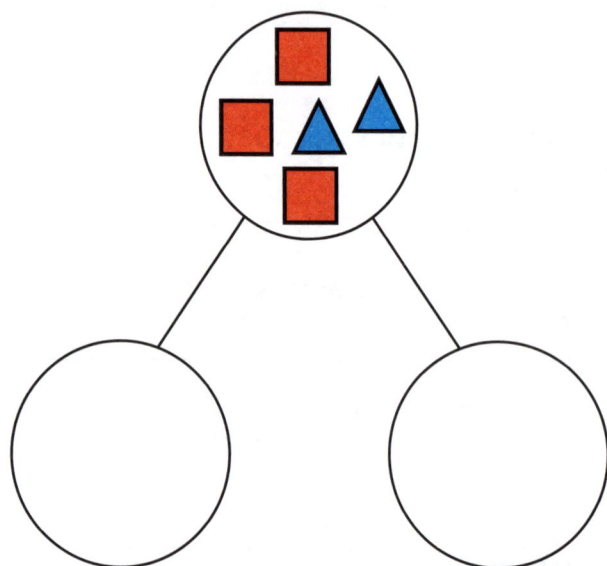

2 Draw counters to complete the part-whole models.

a)   b)

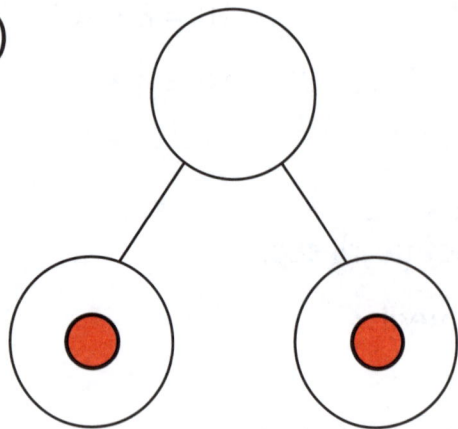   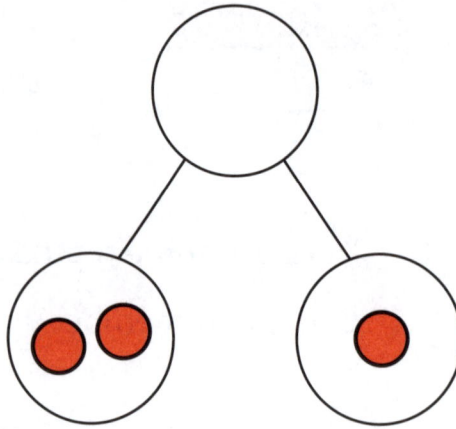

3   Complete the part-whole models and sentences.

a)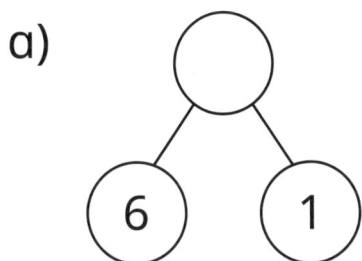

⬜ is a part.

⬜ is a part.

⬜ is the whole.

b)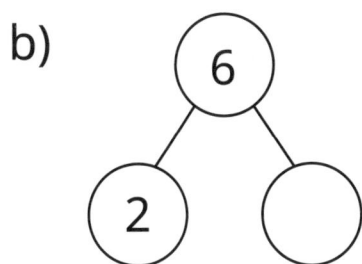

⬜ is a part.

⬜ is a part.

⬜ is the whole.

4   Write an addition sentence to match each part-whole model.

a) 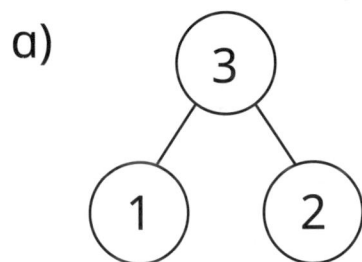   ⬜ + ⬜ = ⬜

b) 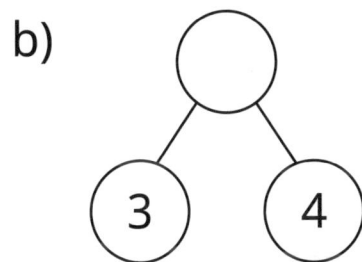   ⬜ + ⬜ = ⬜

5   Eva has drawn a part-whole model.

The whole is 4

The parts are the same.

Draw Eva's part-whole model.

🧠 Think it out

How many different ways can you complete the part-whole model?

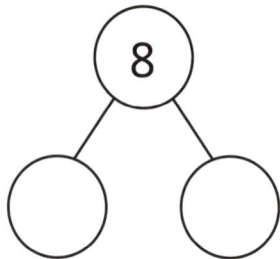

8

I can complete this part-whole model in … different ways.

🏠 Real world maths

What can you find around your home that can be split into parts?

_____

How many parts can it be split into?

_____

How did you find these questions?   🙂   😐   🙁

Addition and subtraction

Date:

Let's practise

1 Write the fact family for each model.

a)
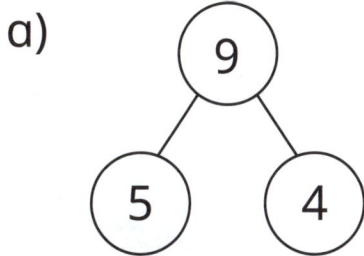

☐ + ☐ = ☐

☐ + ☐ = ☐

☐ = ☐ + ☐

☐ = ☐ + ☐

b)
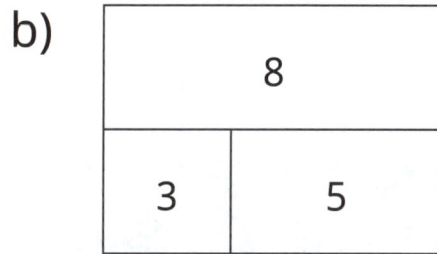

☐ + ☐ = ☐

☐ + ☐ = ☐

☐ = ☐ + ☐

☐ = ☐ + ☐

2 Colour the counters to show the number bonds to 4

● ● ● ● $0 + 4 = 4$

 ☐ + ☐ = 4

 ☐ + ☐ = 4

○ ○ ○ ○ ☐ + ☐ = 4

○ ○ ○ ○ ☐ + ☐ = 4

Number bonds are pairs of numbers added together to make another number.

23

3   Write all the number bonds for 3

_____

_____

4   Match the Numicon Shapes that together make 10

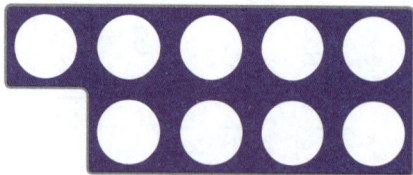

5   Complete the bar models.

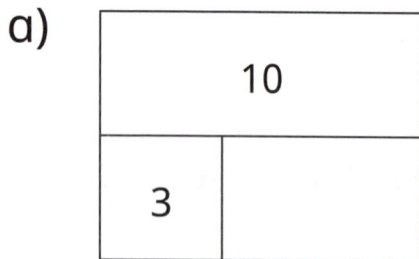

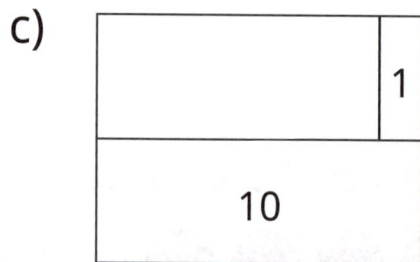

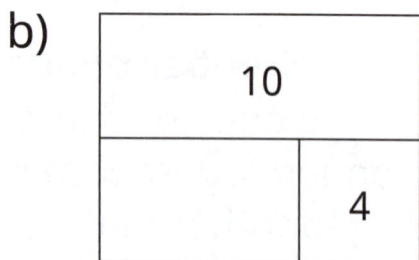

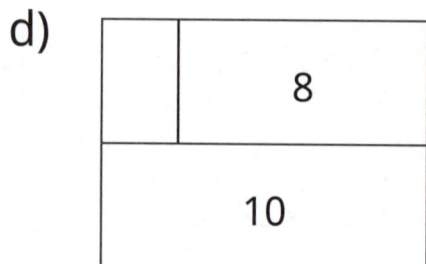

a)

10	
3	

c)

	1
10	

b)

10	
	4

d)

	8
10	

6   Annie has 10 sweets.

She eats 2 sweets and saves the rest.

How many sweets does she save? ☐

💬 Talk it out

Write all the number bonds to 10

_____

_____

Explain how you can make sure you don't miss any.

_____

💬 I will make sure I don't miss any by . . .

💬 I will use . . .

💬 I will check . . .

🧠 Think it out

Max has 10 grapes.

He eats 3 grapes.

He gives 2 grapes to Teddy.

He gives the rest of the grapes to Kim.

Kim eats 2 of the grapes, then gives the rest to Tiny.

How many grapes does Kim give to Tiny?

Use number bonds to help you!

_____

How did you find these questions?   🙂 😐 ☹️

Addition and subtraction

Date:

Let's practise

1 Complete the sentences.

a)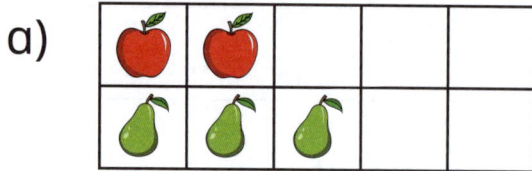

There are ☐ apples.

There are ☐ pears.

There are ☐ pieces of fruit altogether.

b)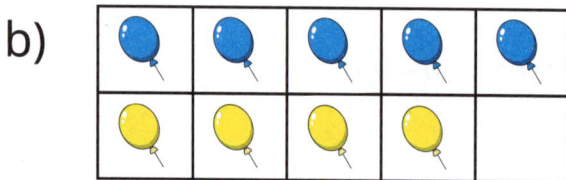

There are ☐ blue balloons.

There are ☐ yellow balloons.

There are ☐ balloons altogether.

What are the parts?
What is the whole?

2 Complete the additions for each ten frame.

a)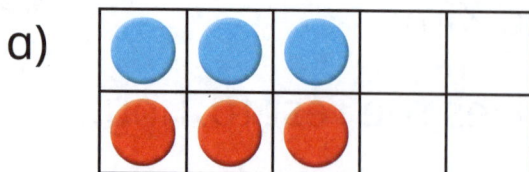

☐ + ☐ = ☐

c)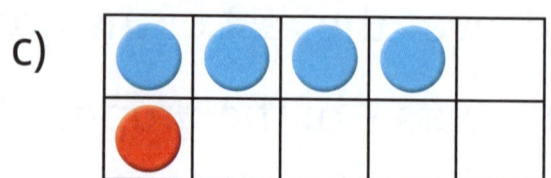

☐ + ☐ = ☐

b)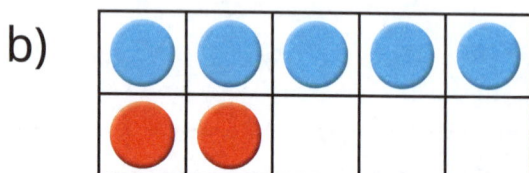

☐ + ☐ = ☐

3 There are 3 sheep and 5 horses in a field.

Draw counters to show how many animals there are altogether. Complete the addition.

$$\boxed{} + \boxed{} = \boxed{}$$

4 3 birds are sitting in a tree.

2 more birds come to sit in the tree.

How many birds are sitting in the tree now? Complete the addition.

$$\boxed{} + \boxed{} = \boxed{}$$

5 Annie has 1 marble.

Teddy gives Annie 7 more marbles.

How many marbles does Annie have now?

How many are there to start with? How many more are added?

$$\boxed{} + \boxed{} = \boxed{}$$

6 Tiny has 2 flowers.

Ron gives Tiny some more flowers.

Tiny now has 6 flowers altogether.

How many flowers does Ron give to Tiny?

$2 + \boxed{} = 6$

27

💬 Talk it out

What word problem could go with this addition?

$$5 + 3 = 8$$

Say it aloud.

Think of another addition problem.

💬 I think the word problem could be …

💬 Another addition problem could be …

💭 Think it out

There are 3 boys and 2 girls on a bus.

1 more boy and 2 more girls get on the bus.

What number bonds can help you?

How many children are now on the bus altogether? ☐

How did you find these questions? 😊 😐 ☹

Addition and subtraction

Date:

Let's practise

1 Complete the part-whole models and additions.

a)
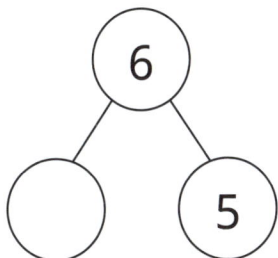

$\boxed{} + 5 = 6$

b)
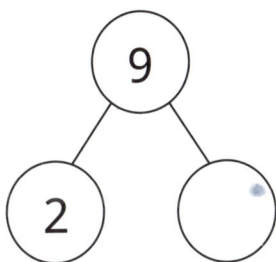

$2 + \boxed{} = 9$

How can you use number bonds to help you?

c)
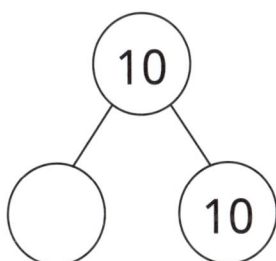

$\boxed{} + 10 = 10$

2 Complete the part-whole models and subtractions.

a)
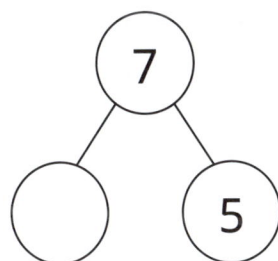

$7 - 5 = \boxed{}$

b)
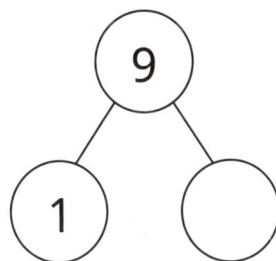

$9 - \boxed{} = \boxed{}$

c)
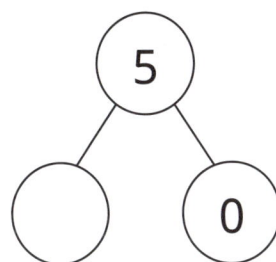

$\boxed{} - \boxed{} = \boxed{}$

29

3   Tiny writes the fact family for the pears and bananas.

$6 + 3 = 9$

$3 + 6 = 9$

$6 - 3 = 9$

$3 - 6 = 9$

Tiny has made some mistakes.

Write the correct fact family for the pears and bananas.

_____

_____

4   There are 5 pets.

3 of them are dogs and 2 of them are cats.

Write the fact family to show the pets.

_____

_____

How do you know you have found all the facts?

Think it out

Here are 3 number cards.

4 **5** **1**

Arrange the cards to make an addition.

☐ + ☐ = ☐

What is the whole?
What are the parts?

Write the fact family.

_____

_____

Talk it out

Eva has completed the part-whole model to show 9 – 5 = 4

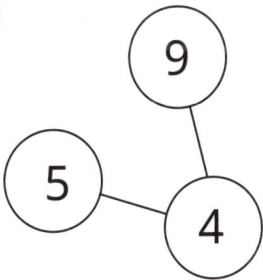

9
5
4

Do you agree with Eva?

Yes, I agree with Eva because ...

No, I do not agree with Eva because ...

To make the part-whole model correct, I would ...

How did you find these questions? 🙂 😐 ☹

Addition and subtraction

Date:

Let's practise

1   Sam has 5 cookies.

She eats 2 cookies.

a)   Cross out the cookies Sam has eaten.

b)   Complete the subtraction 5 – 2 = ☐

2   There are 9 cars in the car park.

3 cars leave the car park.

> How many cars were there at first? How many are left now?

a)   Cross out the cars that leave the car park.

b)   Complete the subtraction ☐ – ☐ = ☐

3   Complete the subtractions.

a)   7 – 1 = ☐

b)   4 – 3 = ☐

c)   2 – 2 = ☐

d)   ☐ = 9 – 5

e)   ☐ = 6 – 4

f)   ☐ = 10 – 7

4   Complete the subtractions to match each number line.

a)

4 – ☐ = ☐

b)
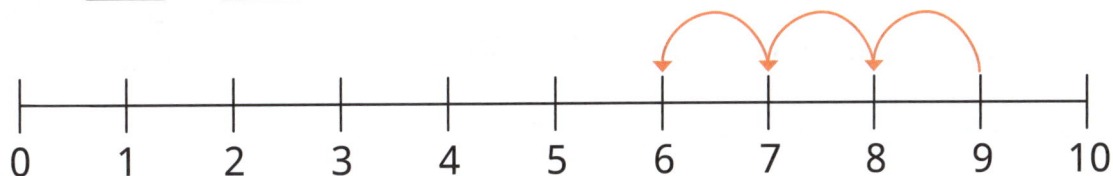

9 – ☐ = ☐

5   Tiny is using a number line to work out 7 – 4

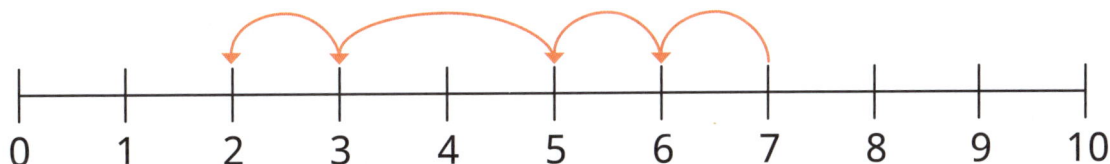

What mistake has Tiny made?

_____.

The answer is 2

6   Show 9 – 7 on this number line.

7   Ron, Mo and Kim are eating cherries.

Ron has 2 fewer cherries than Mo.

Mo has 2 fewer cherries than Kim.

Kim has 6 cherries.

How many cherries do Ron and Mo have?

Ron has ☐ cherries. Mo has ☐ cherries.

33

🏠 Real world maths

Get 10 cubes, counters or other small objects from around your home.

Roll a dice.

Take this amount of objects away.

How many do you have left?

Write a subtraction to match.

☐ – ☐ = ☐

> How many do you need to subtract?

💬 Talk it out

Max writes a subtraction to match the ten frame.

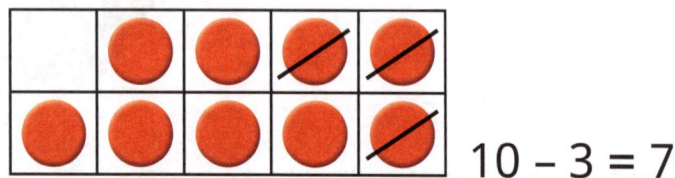

$10 - 3 = 7$

Explain the mistake.

🗨 I have noticed …

🗨 The mistake Max has made is …

🗨 The correct subtraction is …

How did you find these questions?   🙂 😐 🙁

cube	
cylinder	
cuboid	
pyramid	
cone	
sphere	

In this block, we match **3-D shapes** and their names.

rectangle	
circle	
square	
triangle	

We also match **2-D shapes** and their names.

We use shapes to make patterns.

The next shape will be a green square!

Here are some maths words that you'll see.

Can you remember what they mean?

3-D shape   2-D shape   pattern

Shape

Date:

Let's practise

1   Match each shape to its name.

| cylinder | sphere | cuboid | pyramid |

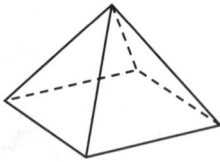

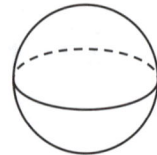

2   Tick the correct name for this shape.

| cone | cube |

3   Match each shape to its name.

| square | circle | triangle | rectangle |

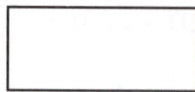

4   Tick the shape that is **not** a triangle.

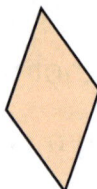

What is the same about the shapes? What is different?

5   Tick all the shapes that are rectangles.

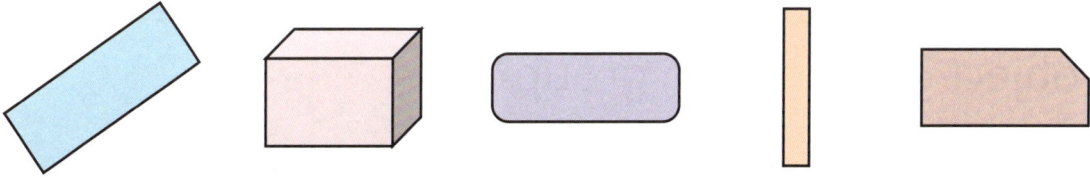

6   Tiny is drawing a square.

Finish Tiny's drawing.

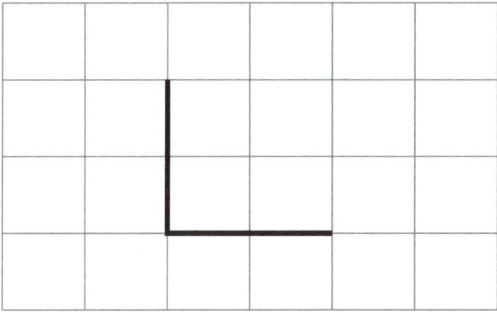

7   Draw the next shape in each pattern.

a)

b)

8   Draw this pattern.

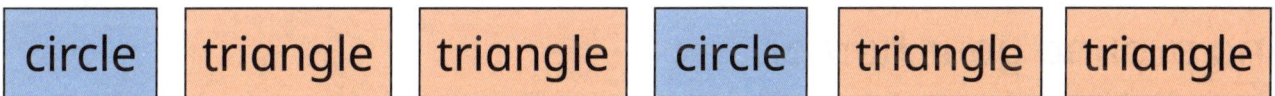

| circle | triangle | triangle | circle | triangle | triangle |

Say the names of the shapes out loud.

 **Talk it out**

Which object goes in each group?

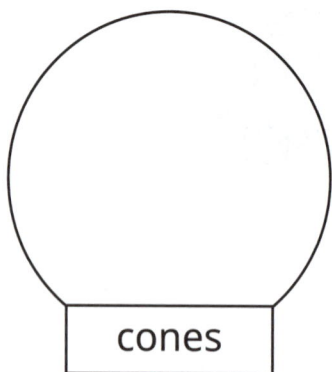 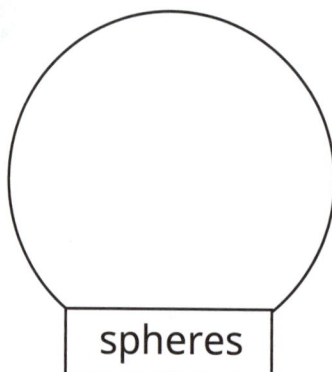 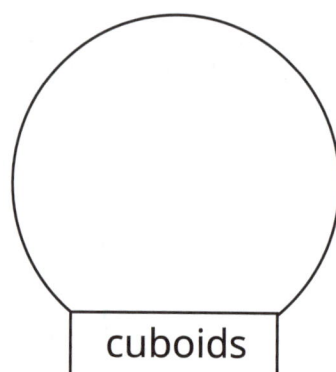

cones

spheres

cuboids

I think this object goes in this group because …

This object is a …
I know this because …

This object is similar to … because …

🏠 **Real world maths**

How many of the shapes you have learned about can you find around your home?

Sort them into groups.

What 2-D shapes can you find? What 3-D shapes can you find?

How did you find these questions?   🙂 😐 🙁

Consolidation

Date:

Let's practise

1 How many dogs are there? ☐

2 a)   Draw 7 counters.

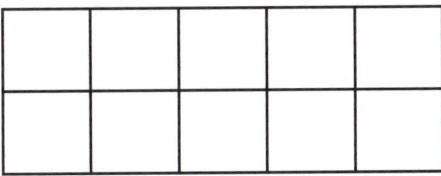

b)   Draw 7 counters in a different way.

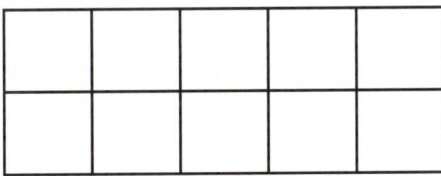

3 Complete the number line.

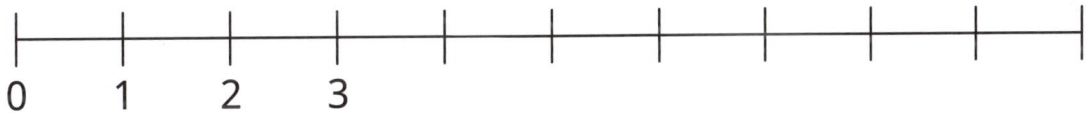

0   1   2   3

4 Colour 6 stars.

5 Complete each bar model.

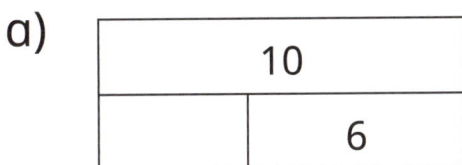

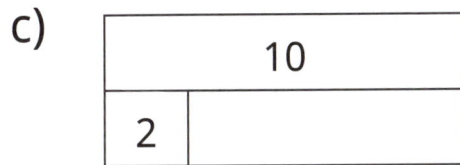

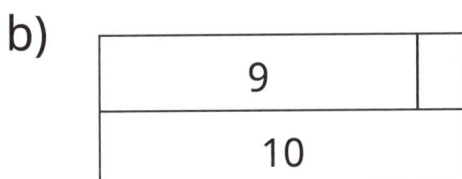

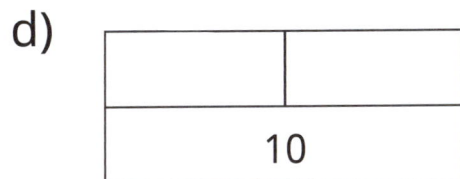

a)

10	
	6

c)

10	
2	

b)

9	
10	

d)

10	

6 Complete the additions.

a) $4 + 5 =$ ⬜   b) $3 + 2 =$ ⬜   c) ⬜ $= 7 + 1$

7 Complete the subtractions.

a) $7 - 2 =$ ⬜   b) $10 - 4 =$ ⬜   c) ⬜ $= 5 - 4$

8 Ron and Mo have some sweets.

Ron

Mo

Use ▨ more ▨ or ▨ fewer ▨ to complete the sentences.

Mo has _____ sweets than Ron.

Ron has _____ sweets than Mo.

9 5 children are playing a game.

1 more child joins the game.

How many children are playing the game now? ⬜

10 Eva has 7 cherries.

Dora has 3 fewer cherries than Eva.

Teddy has 1 more cherry than Dora.

How many cherries does Teddy have? ⬜

How many are there at first? Do you need to add or subtract?

40

🟤 Think it out

How many different ways can you make 10?

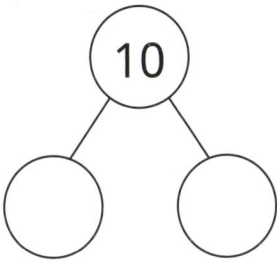

(10)

How can the number bonds to 10 help you?

🟤 Talk it out

Make your own set of number cards like these.

0 1 2 3 4 5 6 7 8 9 10

Place the cards face down, then choose one at random.

Call out the number bond to 10 for your card.

💬 I have picked ...

💬 The number bond to 10 is ...

How did you find these questions? 🙂 😐 🙁

Look back at the place value questions in Block 1.

How many counters are there here? ▢

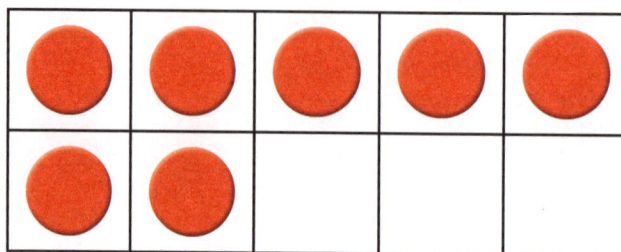

How did you find it?

☺ I get it!   😐 I need a little help.   ☹ I don't get it.

Look back at the part-whole models in Block 2.

Complete the part-whole models.

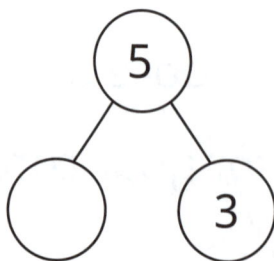

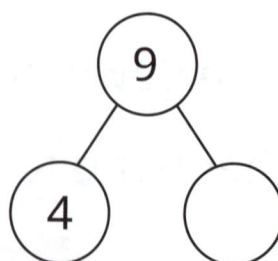

5
◯   3

9
4   ◯

How did you find it?

☺ I get it!   😐 I need a little help.   ☹ I don't get it.

 Do you remember exploring shapes in Block 3?

Match each shape to its name.

sphere

cylinder

pyramid

cuboid

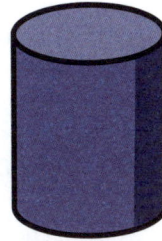

How did you find it?

☺ I get it!

😐 I need a little help.

☹ I don't get it.

 Talk to someone at home about your work this term.
What went well? What do you want to practise?

Spring term
Block 1 Place value

In this block, we **count** up to 20

The missing number here is 17

14	15	16	

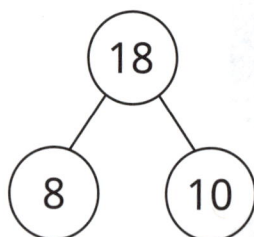

We also use **part-whole models**.

This one shows the **whole** 18 split into the **parts** 8 and 10

We count using **ten frames**.

Here there are 19 counters **in total**.

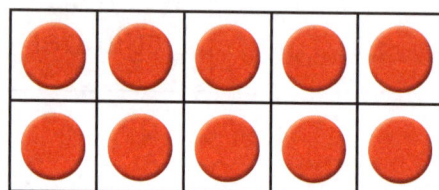

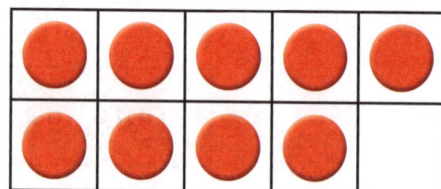

We use **number lines** to find **1 more** and **1 less**.

The circle shows 1 more than 16

The triangle shows 1 less than 16

17 is more than 16. We write this as 17 > 16

15 is less than 16. We write this as 15 < 16

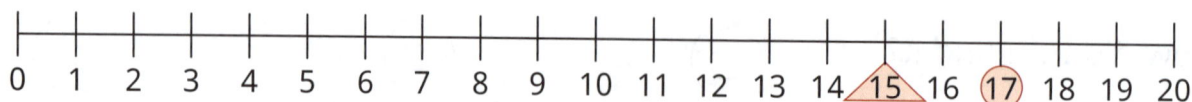

Here are some maths words that you'll see.

Can you remember what they mean?

in total   1 more   1 less   more than   less than

equal to   parts   whole   estimate

44

Place value

Let's practise

1 Complete the number tracks.

a)

10	11	12			

b)

9	10	11					

c)

		13	12		10		

2 Tick the pictures that show 10

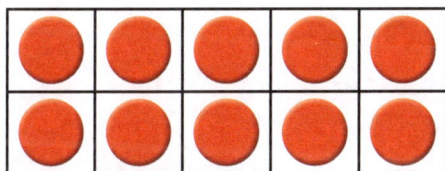 

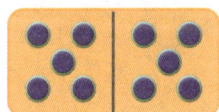

3 Tiny is counting.

> Fourteen, fifteen, seventeen ...

Is Tiny correct? _____

How do you know?

_____

_____

45

4   Complete the part-whole models.

a)
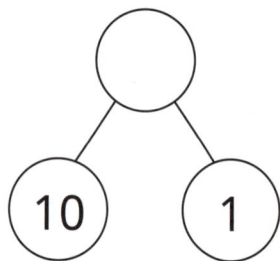

A **part-whole model** shows how a whole number can be split into different parts.

b)
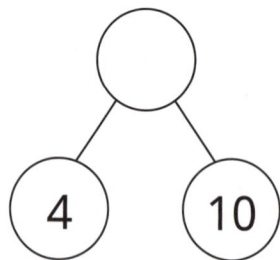

c)
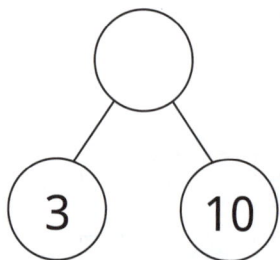

d)
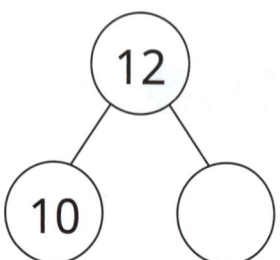

5   Max is counting cubes.

1, 2, 3, ...

How could Max count in a better way?

_____

🏠 Real world maths

Use pieces of pasta, buttons or other small objects you can find at home.

Make each number on the ten frames in a different way.

10   11   12   13   14   15   16

How did you count them?

_____

Ask an adult how many there are.

How did the adult count them?

_____

💭 Think it out

Here are two boxes.

Each box has some pens.

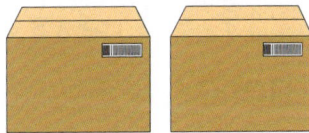

There are 10 pens in total.

How many could be in each box?

Use number bonds to help!

_____

_____

How did you find these questions?   😊   😐   ☹️

47

Place value

Date:

Let's practise

1   Match the pictures to the numbers.

19

17

18

What is the same and what is different about 17, 18 and 19?

2   How many are there?

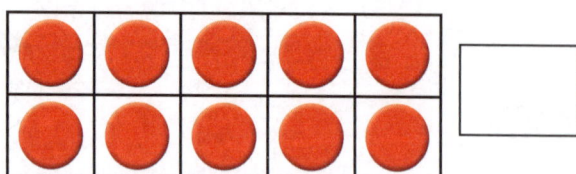

How do you know?

_____

3 Use the number track to complete the sentences.

11	12	13	14	15	16	17	18	19	20

a) 1 more than 11 is ☐

b) 1 less than 15 is ☐

c) 1 more than 16 is ☐

d) 1 more than 19 is ☐

e) 1 less than ☐ is 17

f) 19 is 1 more than ☐

4 Here is a number line.

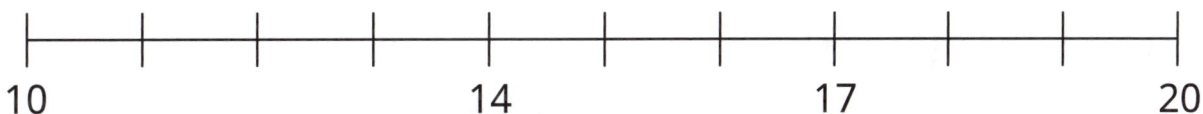

```
├──┼──┼──┼──┼──┼──┼──┼──┼──┼──┤
10          14         17         20
```

a) Complete the number line.

b) Circle fourteen.

c) Draw an arrow to 18 on the number line.

d) Underline twelve.

5 Sam is thinking of a number.

My number has 7 ones and 1 ten.

What number is Sam thinking of? ☐

🏠 Real world maths

Make your own number line from 10 to 20 using string and pieces of paper.

Make each number on the number line in different ways.

10 **11** **12** **13** **14** **15** **16** **17** **18** **19** **20**

> How can number bonds help you?

🧠 Think it out

Max is throwing bean bags at the target.

How can he score 20?

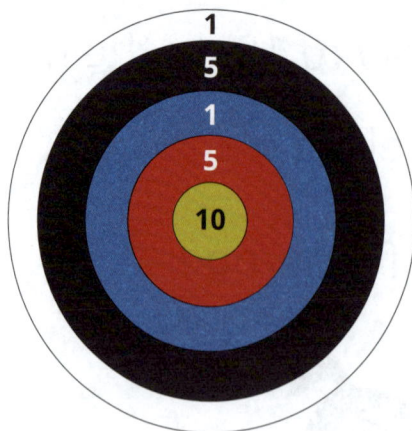

How did you find these questions?   🙂 😐 🙁

Place value

Let's practise

1 Write the numbers the arrows are pointing to.

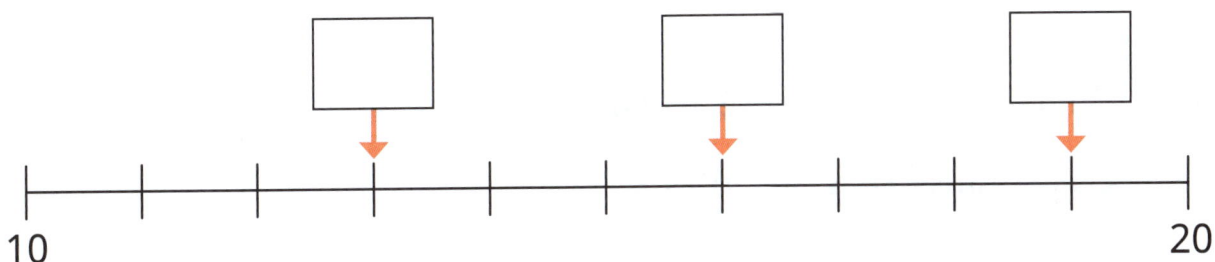

10   20

2 Here is a number line.

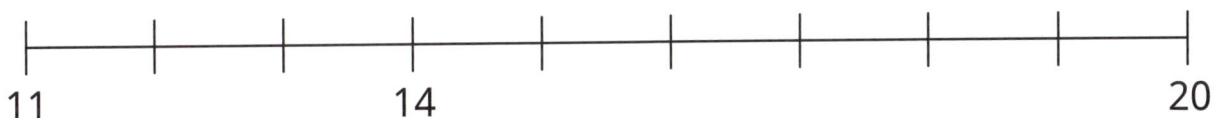

11   14   20

a) Complete the number line.

b) Circle the number that is 1 less than 17

c) Underline the number that is 1 more than 12

d) Draw an arrow to the number that is 1 less than 20

3 Draw an arrow to show the position of each number on the number line.

| 15 | 18 | 12 | 14 |

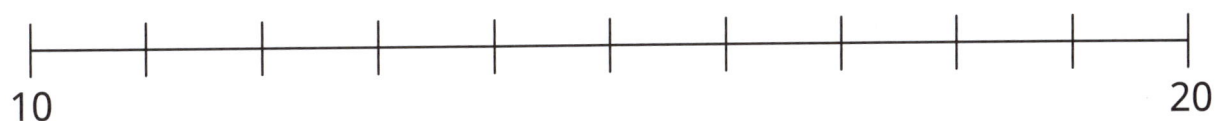

10   20

4 Write <, > or = to compare the numbers.

   a)   14 ◯ 17   c)   eleven ◯ 10

   b)   19 ◯ 18   d)   twenty ◯ 20

5 Write the numbers in order.

   Start with the smallest.

   a)   13, 17, 11

   _____

   b)   20, 10, 16

   _____

   c)   7, 14, 10

   _____

6 Jo is thinking of a number.

   Write all the numbers Jo could
   be thinking of.

   _____

   My number is greater than 13 and less than 18

7 Estimate the number the arrow is pointing to.

   Remember, an **estimate** is a best guess.

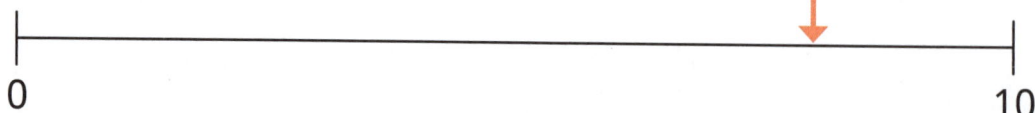

   0   10

💬 Talk it out

Estimate the number the arrow is pointing to.

↓

|————————————————————————————————|
10   20

Why is your answer an estimate?

> 💬 I estimate the arrow is pointing to . . .
> My answer is an estimate because . . .

💭 Think it out

Kim, Ron and Mo are playing a game.

The player with the most points wins.

Ron has 20 points.

Mo has 13 points.

Ron wins the game.

> What numbers are between 13 and 20? What numbers are less than 13?

How many points could Kim have if she comes second?

_____

How many points could Kim have if she comes last?

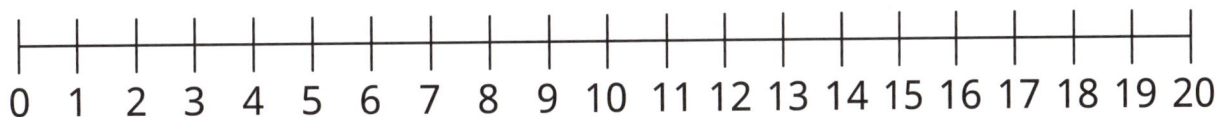

_____

|—+—+—+—+—+—+—+—+—+—+—+—+—+—+—+—+—+—+—+—|
0 1 2 3 4 5 6 7 8 9 10 11 12 13 14 15 16 17 18 19 20

How did you find these questions? 🙂 😐 🙁

53

Block 2 Addition and subtraction

In this block, we **add** and **subtract** numbers within 20

We use **number lines** to help us to find **how many more**.

4 more than 11 is 15

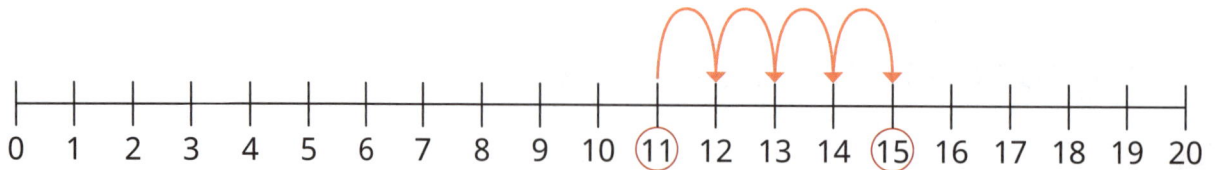

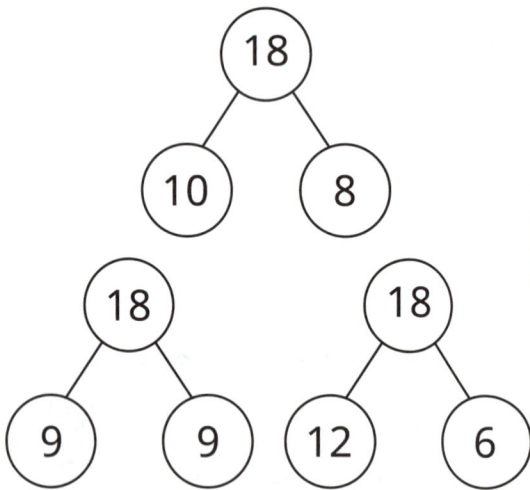

We use **part-whole models** to split numbers up in different ways.

We use **ten frames** to help us **double** numbers.

Here is double 6. There are 12 counters in total. Double 6 is 12

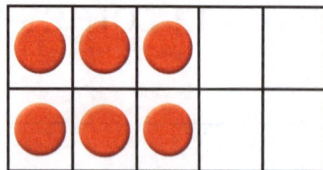

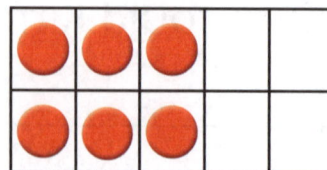

Here are some maths words that you'll see.

Can you remember what they mean?

add   subtract   addition   subtraction   how many more

how many less   parts   whole   double   near double

Addition and subtraction

Let's practise

1   First, there are 8 frogs in a pond.

Then, 5 more frogs get in the pond.

Now, how many frogs are there? ☐

Use the number line to help you.

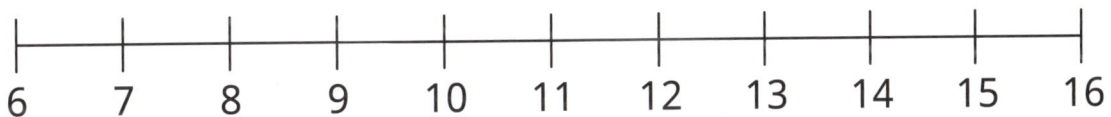

```
├──┼──┼──┼──┼──┼──┼──┼──┼──┼──┤
6    7    8    9   10   11   12   13   14   15   16
```

2   Use the number line to complete the additions.

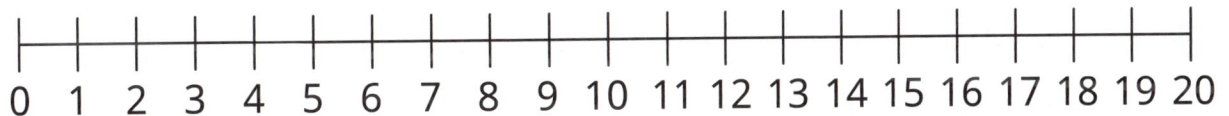

```
├─┼─┼─┼─┼─┼─┼─┼─┼─┼─┼─┼─┼─┼─┼─┼─┼─┼─┼─┼─┤
0  1  2  3  4  5  6  7  8  9 10 11 12 13 14 15 16 17 18 19 20
```

a) $9 + 4 =$ ☐ $4 + 9 =$ ☐

b) $8 + 5 =$ ☐ $5 + 8 =$ ☐

c) $7 + 6 =$ ☐ $6 + 7 =$ ☐

Is it quicker to add 4 to 9 or to add 9 to 4? Is the answer the same?

3   a)   Complete the part-whole models.

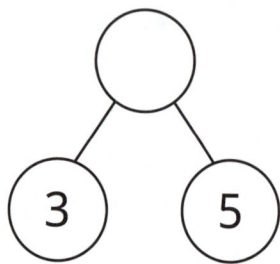

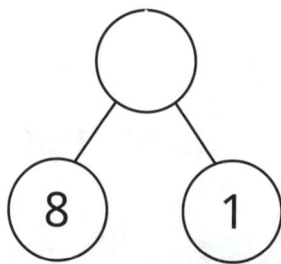

b)   Complete the part-whole models.

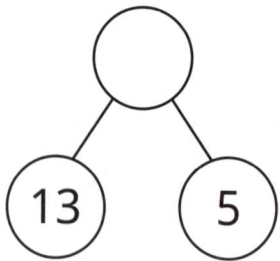

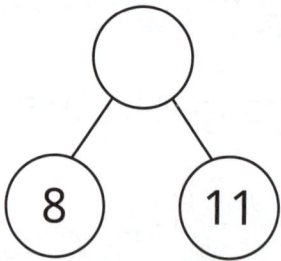

What do you notice?

_____

4   Complete the additions.

a) $14 + 1 = \boxed{}$ d) $\boxed{} = 15 + 4$

b) $5 + 12 = \boxed{}$ e) $\boxed{} = 7 + 11$

c) $3 + 13 = \boxed{}$ f) $12 + \boxed{} = 20$

5   Complete the part-whole model in two different ways.

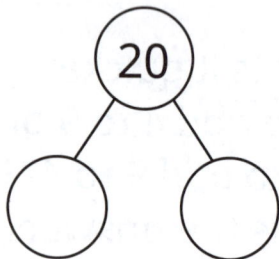

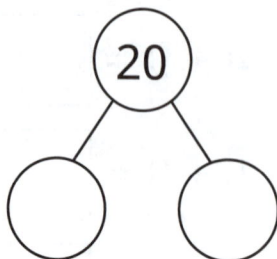

Use number bonds to help!

Are there any other ways you could do it?

_____

🧠 Think it out

Kim and Jack are thinking of a number.

What number could they each be thinking of?

_____

How many answers can you find?

_____

_____

> My number has 1 ten and some ones.

> Kim's number add my number is 20

🏠 Real world maths

Write your own First … Then … Now story for addition.

_____

_____

Ask someone at home to work out the answer.

How did they do it?

_____

💬 First, there were … Then, … Now, there are …

How did you find these questions?   🙂 😐 🙁

Addition and subtraction

Date:

Let's practise

1   Draw counters to show the doubles.

Then complete the sentences.

> Remember, **double** means two lots of something.

a)

Double 4 is ☐

b)

Double 8 is ☐

2   Complete the sentences.

a)   Double 2 is ☐

c)   Double 6 is ☐

b)   Double ☐ is 2

d)   Double ☐ is 6

3   Kim is working out near doubles.

> I can use double 3 to help me work out 3 + 4

Complete the sentences.

3 + 4 = ☐

3 + 4 is equal to double ☐ plus ☐

4   Use near doubles to complete the additions.

Then complete the sentences.

A **near double** is close to a doubles fact.

a)   5 + 6 = ☐

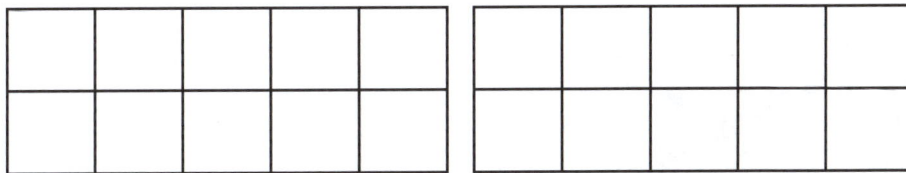

5 + 6 is equal to double ☐ plus ☐

b)   7 + 8 = ☐

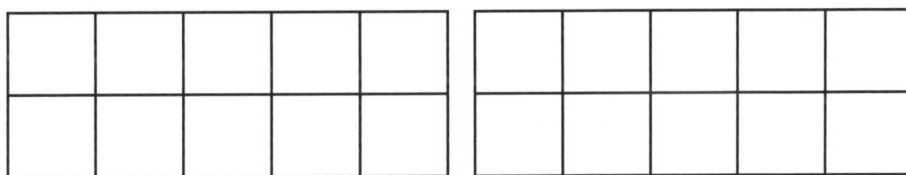

7 + 8 is equal to double ☐ plus ☐

5   Ron is working out 15 – 2

I know
5 – 2 = 3

How does this help?

_____

What is 15 – 2? ☐

6   Kim is thinking of a number.

What number is Kim thinking of?

1 more than double my number is 13

☐

🏠 Real world maths

Use pieces of pasta or buttons to make doubles.

Double 7 is 14

Complete the sentence for each double you make.

Double ☐ is ☐

Now use pieces of pasta or buttons to make near doubles.

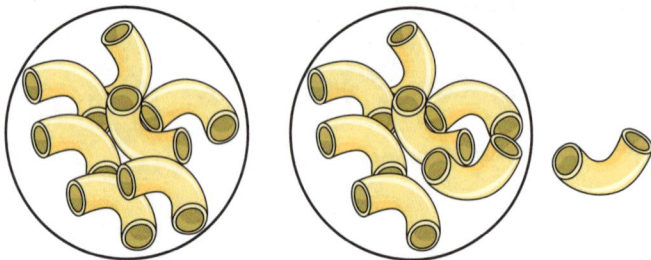

7 + 8 is equal to double 7 plus 1

Complete the sentence for each near double you make.

☐ + ☐ is equal to double ☐ plus ☐

💬 ... is 1 more than ..., so I can work out double ... and then add 1

How did you find these questions?   🙂 😐 🙁

Addition and subtraction

Date:

Let's practise

1   Draw jumps on the number lines to complete the subtractions.

a)

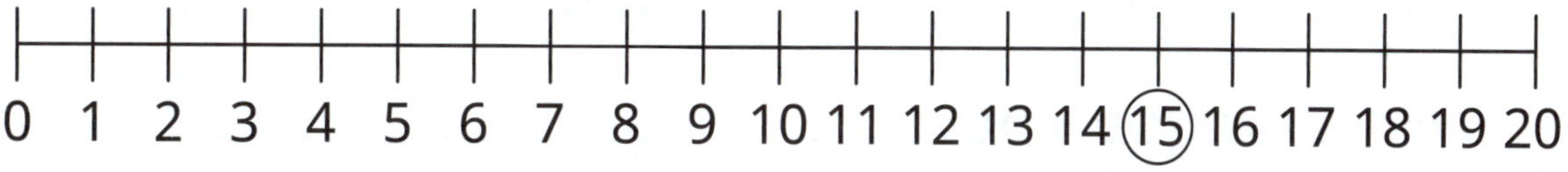

0 1 2 3 4 5 6 7 8 9 10 11 12 13 14 (15) 16 17 18 19 20

15 – 4 = ☐

b)

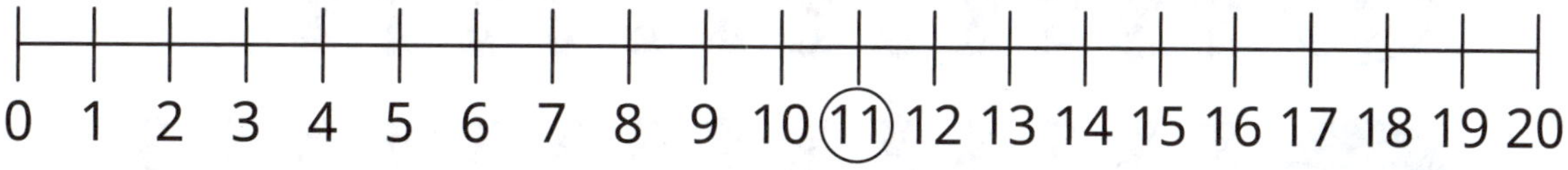

0 1 2 3 4 5 6 7 8 9 10 (11) 12 13 14 15 16 17 18 19 20

11 – 4 = ☐

c)

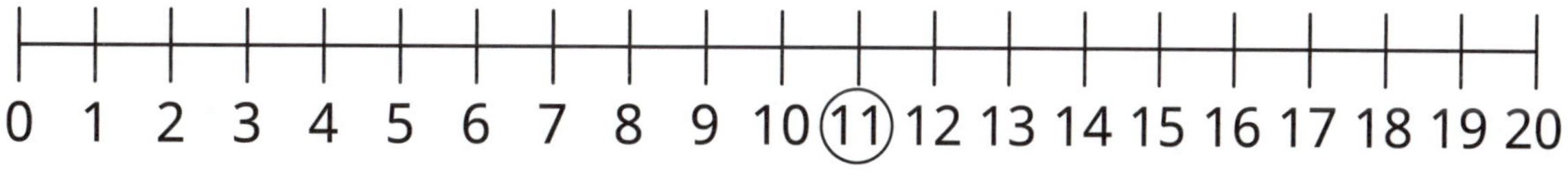

0 1 2 3 4 5 6 7 8 9 10 (11) 12 13 14 15 16 17 18 19 20

11 – 6 = ☐

d)

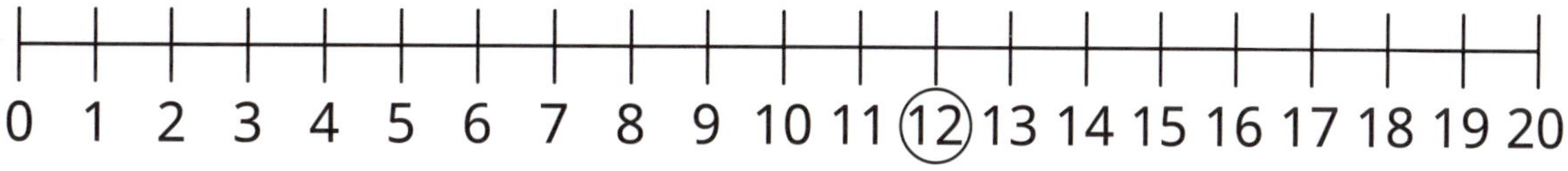

0 1 2 3 4 5 6 7 8 9 10 11 (12) 13 14 15 16 17 18 19 20

12 – 5 = ☐

2 Ben and Sam have some marbles.

Ben

Sam

How many more marbles does Ben have than Sam? ☐

How do you know? _____

3 Jack and Kim have some sweets.

How many more sweets does

Kim have than Jack? ☐

4 Write the fact family for this part-whole model.

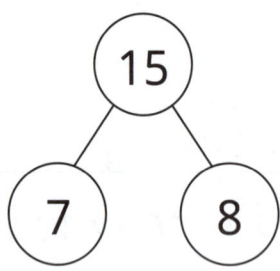

15

7   8

What is the
same and what
is different?

_____

_____

Real world maths

Get a pile of buttons or counters.

Split them into two parts.

Draw a part-whole model to show your parts.

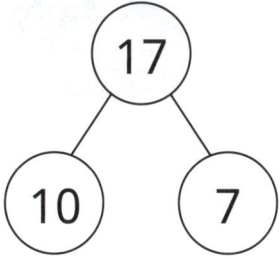

17

10   7

Write 4 number sentences to match your part-whole model.

10 + 7 = 17   17 − 10 = 7

7 + 10 = 17   17 − 7 = 10

_____

_____

What addition sentences can you write? What subtraction sentences can you write?

How did you find these questions?   😊   😐   ☹

In this block, we **count** to 50

We use base 10 to help us.
This number is 47

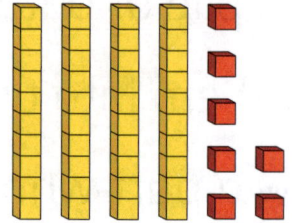

We count in **tens** and in **ones**.

10, 20, 30

1, 2, 3, 4, 5, 6

We use **part-whole models** to help us split numbers into different parts.

This model shows 38 split into 3 tens and 8 ones.

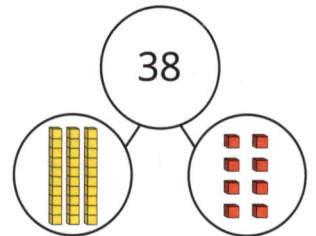

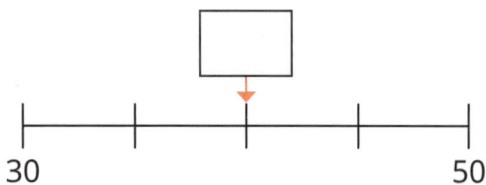

38

We also find missing numbers on **number lines**.
I **estimate** the arrow is pointing to 40

30   50

Here are some maths words that you'll see.

Can you remember what they mean?

part   whole   tens   ones   estimate   count

Place value

Let's practise

1 Complete the number tracks.

a)

21	22			

b)

42	41			

2 a) Complete the number track.

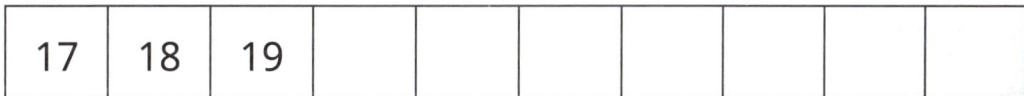

17	18	19							

b) What number comes before 17?

c) What number comes after 49?

What number comes next?

3 How many triangles are there in each group?

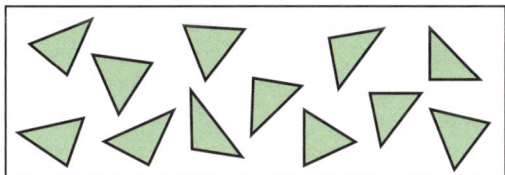

Which were easier to count?

4   Complete the sentences.

There are ☐ groups of 10 apples.

There are ☐ apples.

Choose if you count in ones or tens.

5   What number is shown? ☐

How did you count?

_____

6   Complete the sentences to describe the number.

There are ☐ tens and ☐ ones.

The number shown is ☐

7   Jack has 5 base 10 pieces.

He has some tens and some ones.

What number could Jack have?

☐

Is there more than one possible number?

🏠 Real world maths

Get a pile of small objects, such as dried pasta, counters or building blocks.

Arrange the objects to make them easier to count.

How did you do it?

_____

Ask someone else to count some objects.

Did they arrange them before they counted?

_____

Could using rows help?

💭 Think it out

Pencils come in packs of 10

Ron has 2 packs of pencils.

Dora has 1 pack of pencils.

Max has 3 single pencils.

How many pencils do they have in total? ☐

10

How many tens and how many ones?

How did you find these questions?   🙂 😐 ☹

Place value

Let's practise

1 Draw the missing parts to complete the part-whole models.

a)

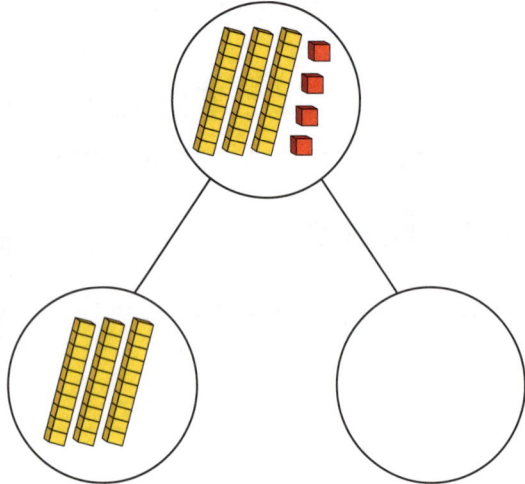

b)

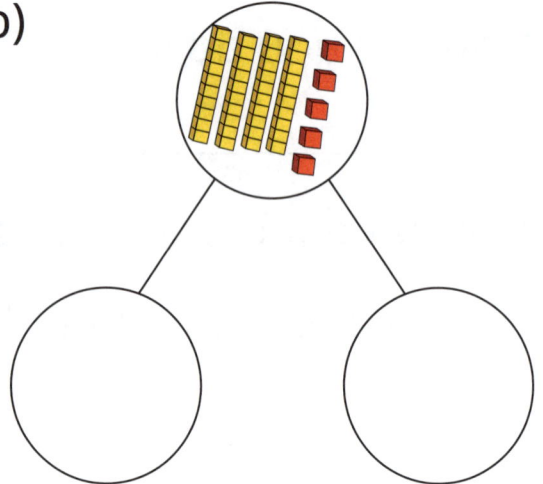

2 Complete the sentences to describe the part-whole model.

[ ] is the whole.

[ ] is a part.

[ ] is a part.

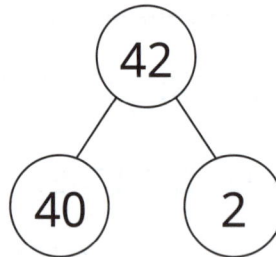

3 Complete the sentences.

a) 37 has [ ] tens and [ ] ones.

b) [ ] has 2 tens and 9 ones.

4 Complete the number line.

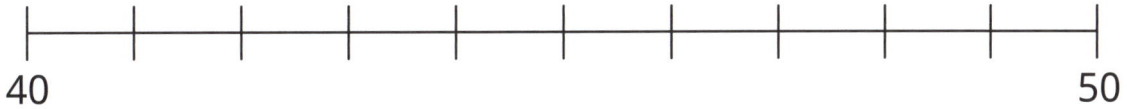

40   50

5

The missing number is 21

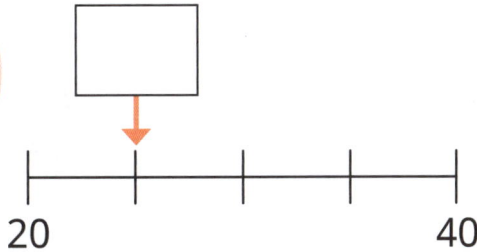

20   40

How much is each jump on this number line?

Do you agree with Tiny? _____

Explain your answer.

_____

6 Draw an arrow to estimate where 25 is on the number line.

Remember, an **estimate** is a best guess.

20   30

7 Complete the sentences.

a)   1 more than 27 is [ ]

b)   1 less than 32 is [ ]

c)   1 _____ than 30 is 29

d)   1 more than [ ] is 46

💬 Talk it out

Here are some number lines.

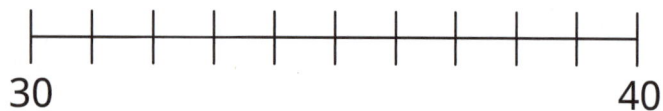

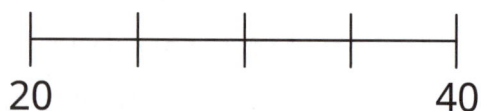

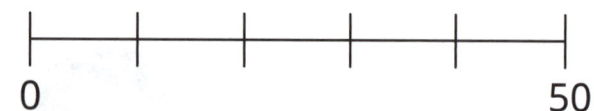

30 |———————————————————| 40

20 |———————————| 40

0 |———————————| 50

> Where does each number line start? Where does each number line end?

Estimate where 37 would go on each line.

Explain your reasons.

_____

_____

_____

💬 I estimate that 37 is here because ....

🧠 Think it out

Which is greater, 4 tens or 4 ones?

_____

_____

How did you find these questions?   🙂 😐 🙁

Block 4 Length and height

In this block, we explore **length** and **height** by **comparing** objects.
The stripy ribbon is **longer** than the plain ribbon.

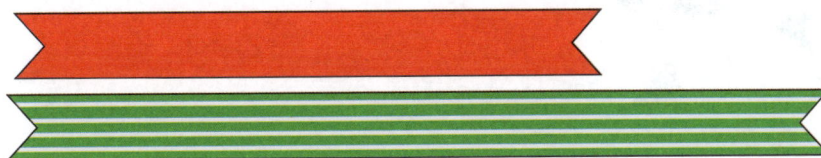

We use cubes to **measure** objects.
This pencil is 5 cubes long.

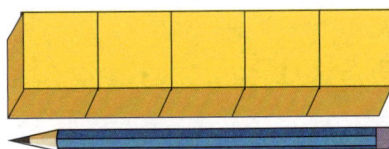

We also use **rulers** to measure objects in **centimetres**.
I have measured this crayon. It is 7 cm long.

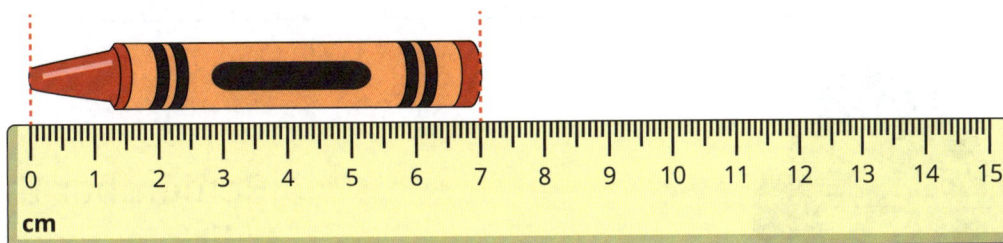

Here are some maths words that you'll see.
Can you remember what they mean?

longer   taller   shorter   centimetres   cm   ruler

compare   measure

Length and height

Date:

Let's practise

1   Tick the shorter tree.

2   Tick the longer train.

3   Use the words to complete the sentences about the flower and the tree.

| taller | longer | shorter |

Remember that **taller** is used for height and **longer** is used for length.

The tree is _____ than the flower.

The flower is _____ than the tree.

4

The red ribbon is taller than the blue ribbon.

What word should Tiny use instead of **taller**? _____

5   How tall is each object?

a)

The teddy is ☐ cubes tall.

Where do you need to start/end measuring?

b)

The juice is ☐ cubes tall.

6

The pencil is 4 cubes long.

Do you agree with Rosie? _____
Explain your answer.

_____

🏠 Real world maths

Use cubes or building bricks to measure objects around your home.

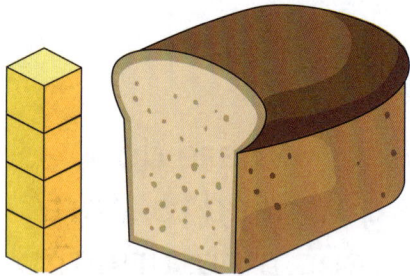

Remember to use cubes or bricks that are all the same size!

Record what you measure.

Object	Number of cubes/bricks

🧠 Think it out

Find something taller and shorter than you in your home.

💬 … is taller than me.

💬 … is shorter than me.

How did you find these questions?   🙂 😐 🙁

Length and height

Let's practise

1   Draw an arrow to show 9 cm.

> Remember, **cm** is short for centimetres.

2   How long is each object?

a)

☐ cm

b)

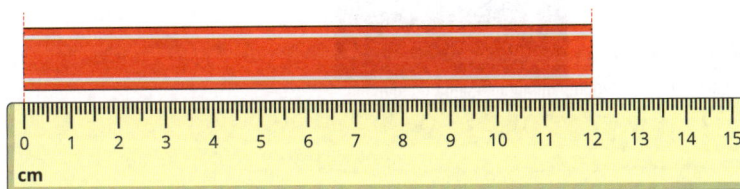

☐ cm

c)

> Remember to start measuring at 0 cm.

☐ cm

75

3 How tall is Tiny?

[ ] cm

4 How long is the leaf?

The leaf is [ ] cm long.

5

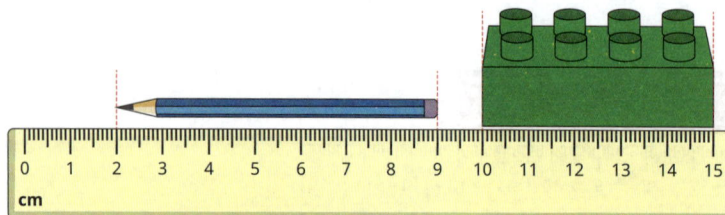

a) Use longer or shorter to complete
    the sentence.

    The pencil is _____ than the brick.

b) Complete the sentences.

    The pencil is [ ] cm long.

    The brick is [ ] cm long.

Which object
is longer or
shorter? How
do you know?

    The _____ is 2 cm shorter than the _____.

🏠 Real world maths

Which objects can you find in your home that measure these lengths?

- 4 cm _____

- 10 cm _____

- 12 cm _____

- 15 cm _____

Remember to position your ruler carefully!

☁ Think it out

How many different length facts can you find in the image?

What number facts do you know that could help?

_____

_____

_____

How did you find these questions?   😊   😐   ☹

77

Block 5 Mass and volume

In this block, we explore **mass**. We **compare** objects using the words **heavier** and **lighter**.

The melon is **heavier** than the banana.

The banana is **lighter** than the melon.

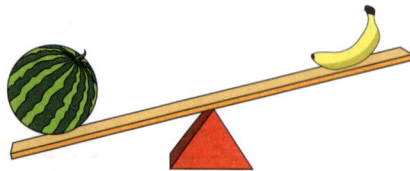

We use cubes to **measure** the mass of objects.

This apple has a mass of 5 cubes.

We also explore **volume**. We **compare** volume using the words **full** and **empty**.

I have one cup that is full of juice and one cup that is empty.

full   empty

We compare the **capacity** of different containers.

The capacity of the mug is **greater than** the capacity of the egg cup.

Here are some maths words that you'll see.

Can you remember what they mean?

mass   lighter   heavier   equal to   full   compare

empty   nearly full   nearly empty   volume   capacity

Mass and volume

Let's practise

1   Use the words to describe each picture.

heavier   lighter

a)

Remember, the heavier object is lower on the balance scale.

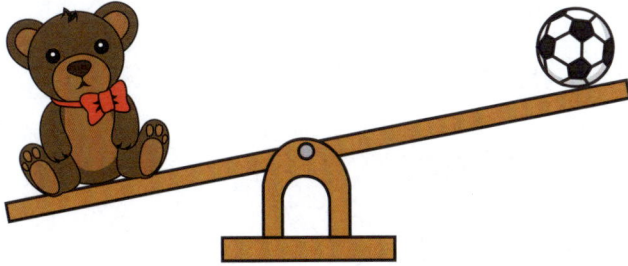

The teddy is _____ than the football.

b)

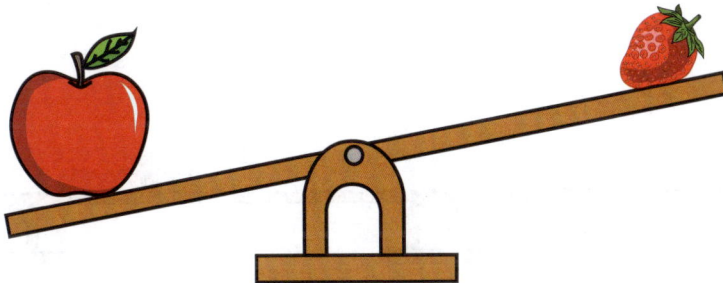

The apple is _____ than the strawberry.

2   Tick the correct picture.

The cube is heavier than the cone.

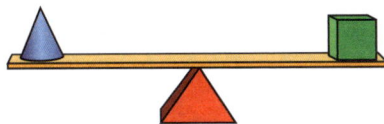

3   What is the mass of the pear?

The mass of the pear is _____.

4   A triangle has a mass of 3 cubes.

A circle has a mass of 4 cubes.

A square has a mass of 5 cubes.

Draw the shapes in the correct place.

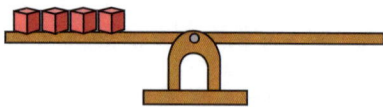

5

a)   Tick the lightest object.

b)   Which object has a mass of 5 cubes?

_____

🧠 Think it out

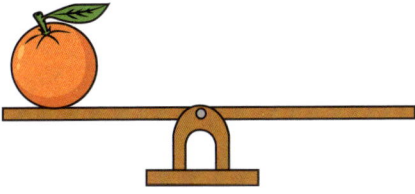

Some odd numbers are 1, 3, 5, 7 and 9.

Use the clues to draw the correct number of cubes.

- The mass of the orange is lighter than 7 cubes.

- The mass of the orange uses an odd number of cubes.

- The mass of the orange is heavier than 3 cubes.

💬 Talk it out

Choose some objects in your home and use the words to talk about their mass.

mass   heavier   lighter   equal to

If you don't have any scales, just have a guess and see if an adult agrees with you.

If you do have scales, guess first and then check if you were correct.

💬 I think the mass of the . . . is heavier/lighter than the mass of the . . .

💬 I think the mass of the . . . is equal to the mass of the . . .

💬 Do you agree?

How did you find these questions? 🙂 😐 ☹️

81

Mass and volume

Date:

Let's practise

1   Colour to show the amounts.

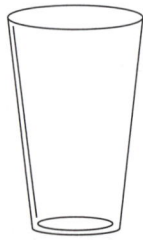 

full   nearly empty

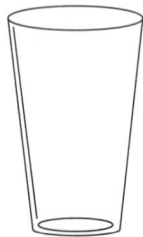 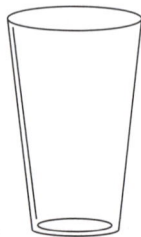

empty   nearly full

Remember, **full** means there is no more space in the cup. **Empty** means there is nothing in the cup.

2   Tick the glass that has the most juice.

   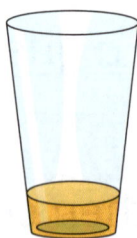   

3

My bottle is full.

Do you agree with Tiny? Explain your answer.

_____

4 Write <, > or = to compare the capacity of
the containers.

Capacity means
how much a
container can hold.

5 3 small glasses fill 1 tall glass.

a) How many small glasses fill 2 tall glasses?

b) Ron has 5 full tall glasses of water.

How many small glasses can he fill?

🏠 Real world maths

How many cups of water fill a pan?

Remember to fill your cup to the top each time!

Compare your answer with others in your class.

Why might your answer be different?

_____

🧠 Think it out

A bottle holds 5 glasses of juice.

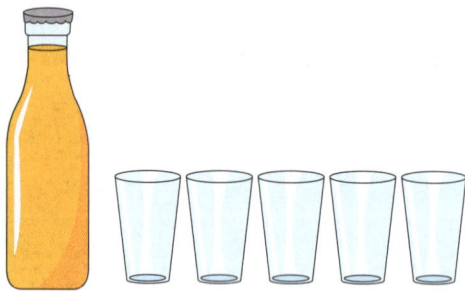

How could counting in 5s help?

A barrel holds 7 bottles of juice.

How many glasses of juice can fit into the barrel?

How did you find these questions?   🙂 😐 🙁

Time to reflect

Look back at the place value questions in Block 1.

Complete this number line.

Circle 1 less than 13

Underline 1 more than 14

13   15   18   20

How did you find it?

☺ I get it!   😐 I need a little help.   ☹ I don't get it.

Do you remember measuring objects in Block 4?

How long is this pencil? ☐ cm

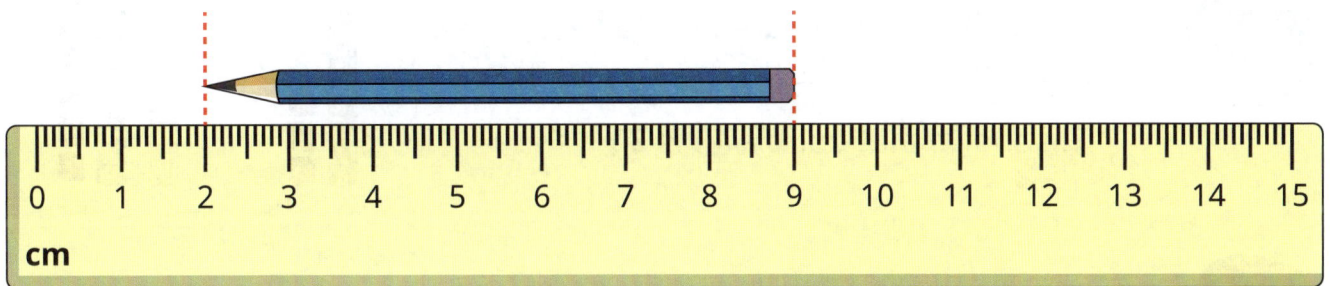

How did you find it?

☺ I get it!   😐 I need a little help.   ☹ I don't get it.

Talk to someone at home about your work this term.
What went well? What do you want to practise?

Summer term
Block 1 Multiplication and division

In this block, we look at **multiplication** and **division**.

We count in 2s, 5s and 10s using **number lines**.

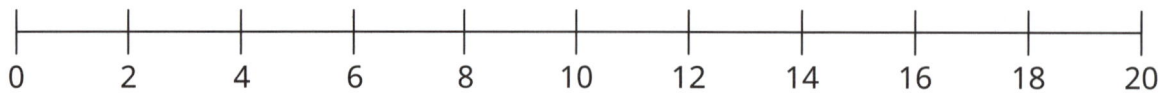

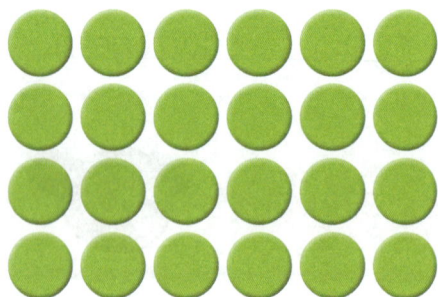

```
0   2   4   6   8   10  12  14  16  18  20
```

```
0   5   10  15  20  25  30  35  40
```

```
0   10  20  30  40  50
```

We use **rows** and **columns** to help find **how many altogether**.
There are 4 rows of counters.
There are 6 counters in each row.
There are 24 counters altogether.

We practise **doubling** by using **base 10** to add a number to itself.

This shows that double 13 is 26

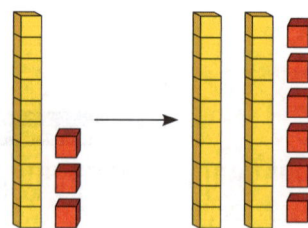

Here are some maths words that you'll see.
Can you remember what they mean?

rows   columns   how many altogether   double   doubling

sharing   grouping   equal   multiplication   division

Multiplication and division

Date:

Let's practise

1 Write the numbers.

a)

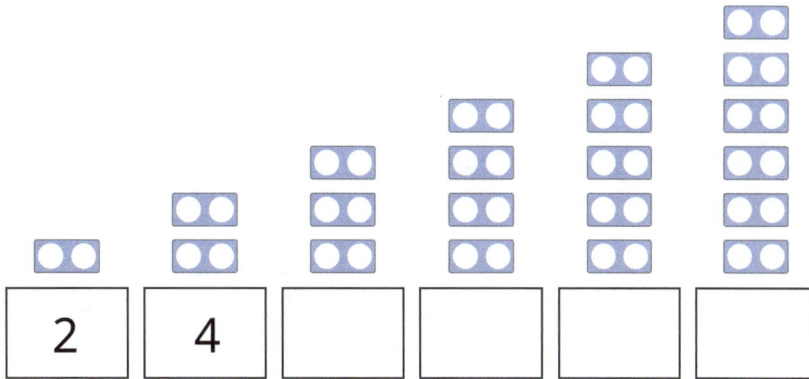

| 2 | 4 | | | | |

b)

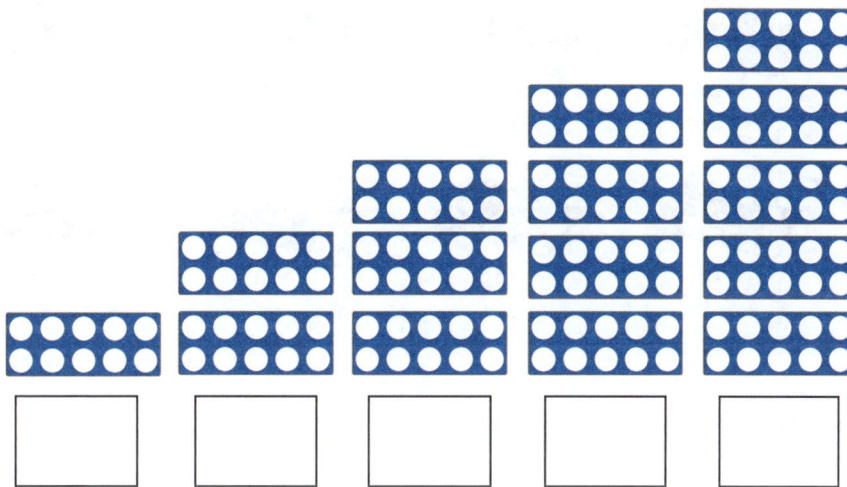

c)

2 Circle 16 shoes.

3 Colour 30 dots.

4 Circle 60 marbles.

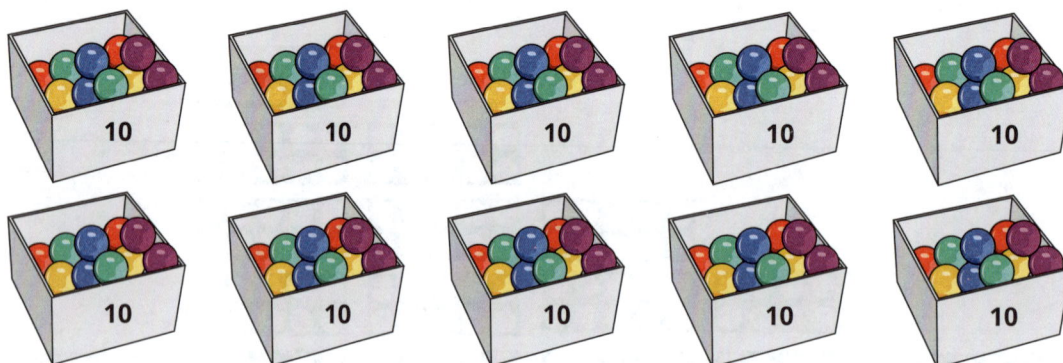

10 10 10 10 10

10 10 10 10 10

5 Complete the number lines.

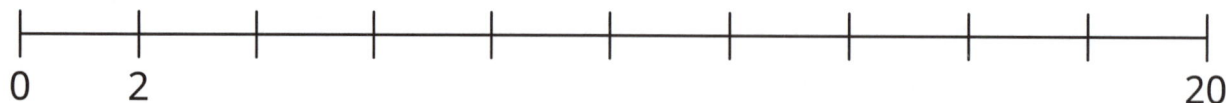

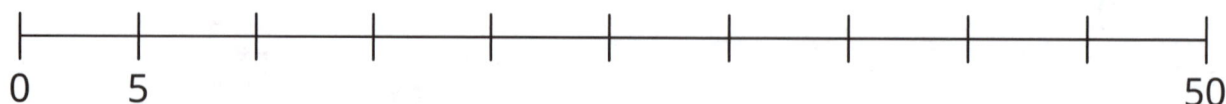

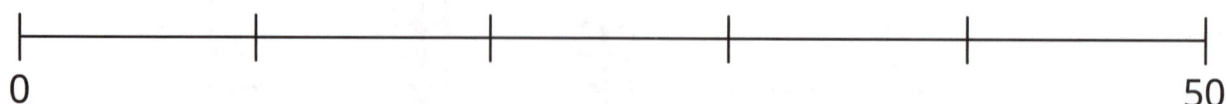

0   2   20

0   5   50

0   50

Write the numbers that are on all 3 number lines.

_____

🏠 Real world maths

How many socks do you have?

Make sure you count them in pairs.

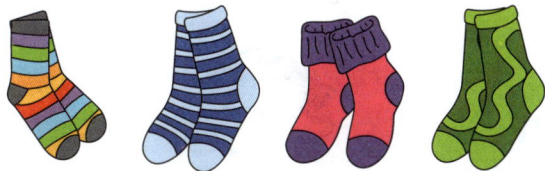

2, 4, 6, 8 ...

💭 Think it out

Max is counting in 2s to 20

Jo is counting in 5s to 20

What numbers will they both say?

_____

What do you notice?

_____

_____

How did you find these questions?   🙂   😐   ☹️

Multiplication and division   Date:

Let's practise

1   Tick the equal groups.

> Remember, **equal** means the same amount.

2   Complete the sentences.

a)

There are ☐ equal groups of ☐

☐ + ☐ + ☐ + ☐ = ☐

There are ☐ altogether.

b)

There are ☐ equal groups of ☐

☐ + ☐ + ☐ + ☐ + ☐ = ☐

There are ☐ altogether.

3   How many rows of cubes are there? ☐

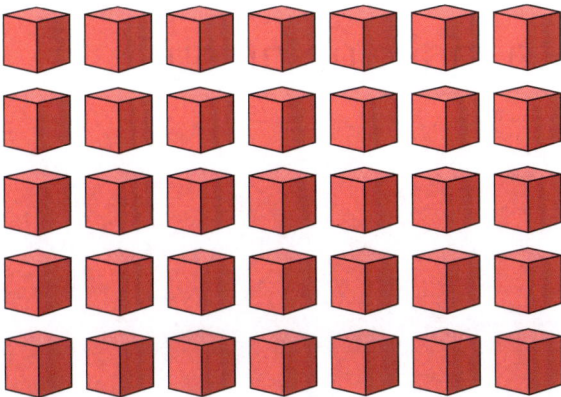

Rows go across and columns go up and down.

4   How many columns of apples are there? ☐

5   Complete the sentences.

There are ☐ rows of counters.

There are ☐ counters in each row.

There are ☐ counters altogether.

🏠 Real world maths

Use pieces of pasta or buttons to make an array.

Complete the sentences to describe your array.

There are ☐ rows.

There are ☐ in each row.

There are ☐ altogether.

There are ☐ columns.

There are ☐ in each column.

There are ☐ altogether.

Remember, an **array** is a way of arranging things in rows and columns.

What do you notice?

_____

How did you find these questions?   🙂   😐   🙁

Multiplication and division

Date:

Let's practise

1 Tick the pictures that show doubles.

2 Use the pictures to complete the sentences.

Remember, **doubling** is adding a number to itself.

a)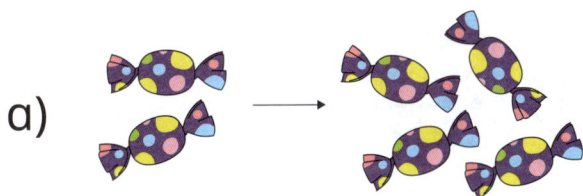

Double 2 is ⬜

b)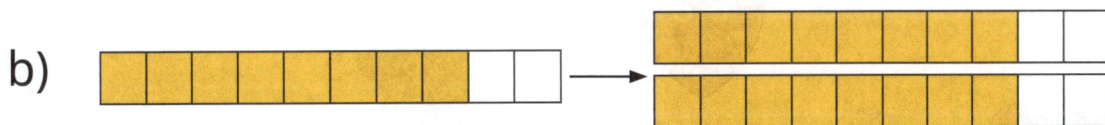

Double 8 is ⬜

c) Double 10 is ⬜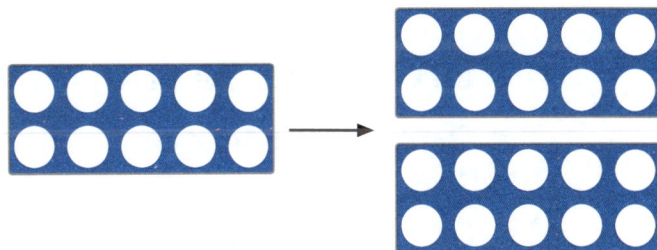

d) Double 14 is ⬜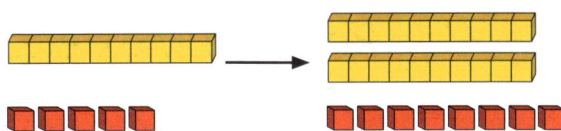

3 Here are some grapes.

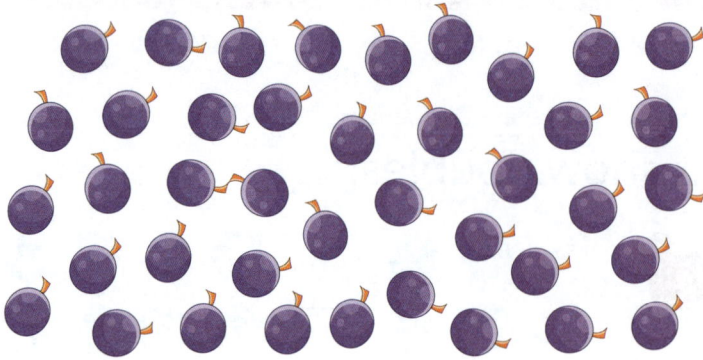

a) Circle groups of 5 grapes.

b) Complete the sentence.

There are ☐ equal groups with 5 in each group.

4 Ron and Max have some stickers.

a) Draw lines to share the stickers equally between Ron and Max.

b) Complete the sentences.

Ron and Max each get ☐ stickers.

☐ shared equally between 2 is ☐

🏠 Real world maths

Get 30 pieces of pasta.

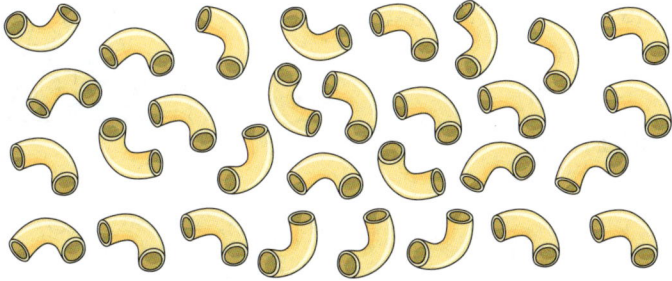

Put the pasta into groups of 5

Complete the sentence.

There are ⬜ equal groups with ⬜ in each group.

Now share the pasta equally into 5 groups.

Complete the sentence.

There are ⬜ equal groups with ⬜ in each group.

What do you notice?

_____

_____

💬 I notice that there are …

How did you find these questions?   🙂 😐 🙁

In this block, we look at **fractions**.

I've drawn a line to split this triangle in **half**.

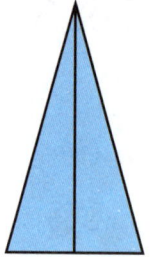

We use **number bonds** to help find one half of a set of objects.

One half of 8 is 4

4 + 4 = 8

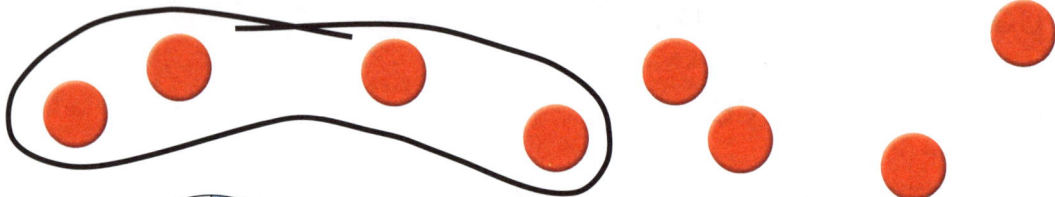

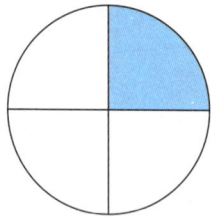

In this block, we also find **quarters**.

I've coloured one quarter of this circle.

We use **number bonds** to help find one quarter of a set of objects.

One quarter of 16 is 4

4 + 4 + 4 + 4 = 16

Here are some maths words that you'll see.

Can you remember what they mean?

fraction   half   quarter   equal

unequal   number bonds

Fractions

Date:

Let's practise

1 Tick the cake that is cut in half.

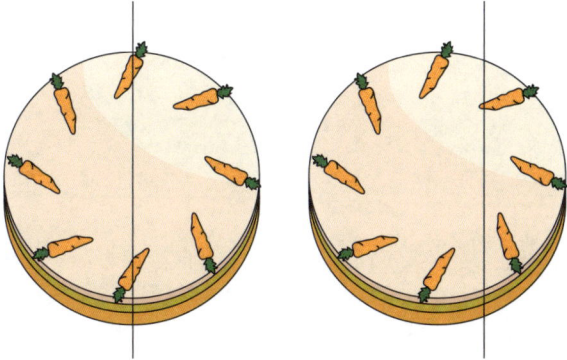

Remember, each half needs to be the same size!

2 Colour one half of each shape.

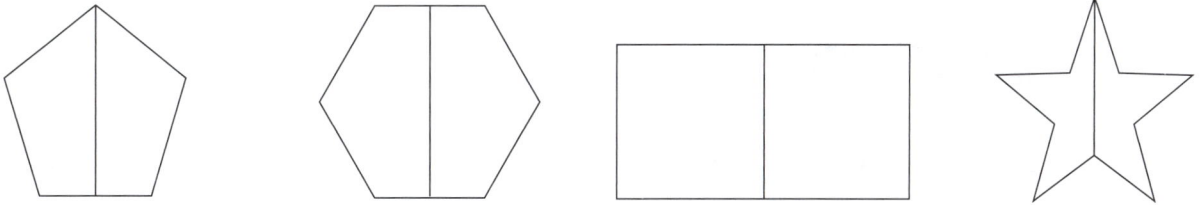

3 Draw a line to split the shapes in half.

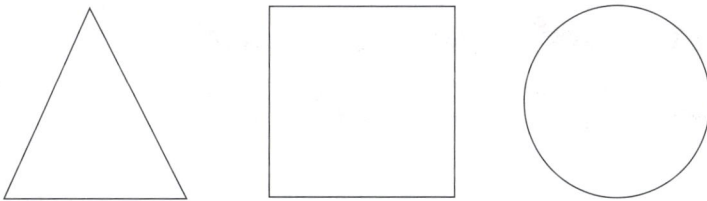

Remember to use a ruler to draw the lines.

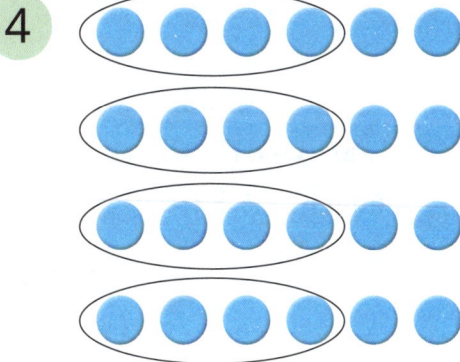

4

I have circled half of the counters.

Do you agree with Tiny? _____
Explain your answer.

_____

5   Circle one half of each set of objects.

Then complete the sentences.

a)

One half of 10 is ☐

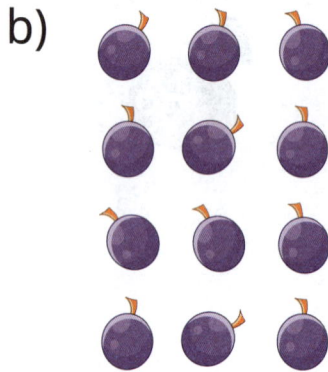

b)

One half of 12 is ☐

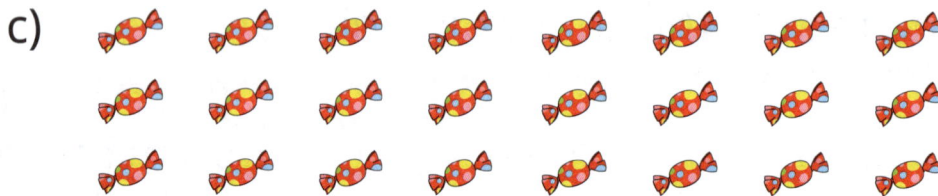

c)

One half of 24 is ☐

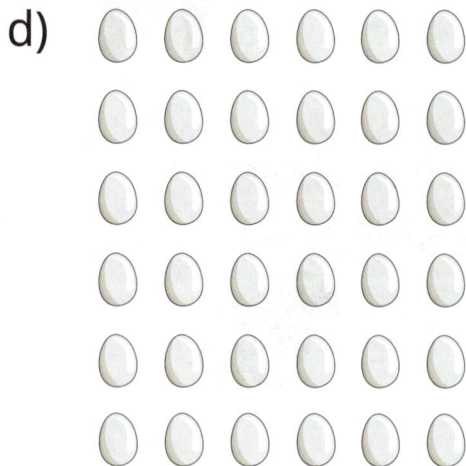

d)

Use number
bonds to help!

One half of 36 is ☐

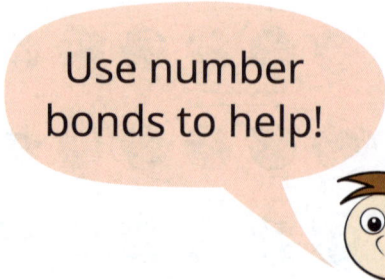

🏠 Real world maths

Use some objects around your home to find one half of different amounts.

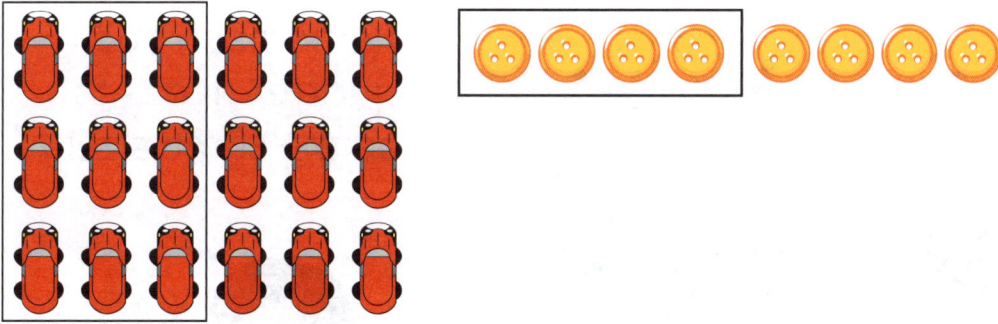

💭 Think it out

Cut some shapes out of pieces of paper.

Fold them in half.

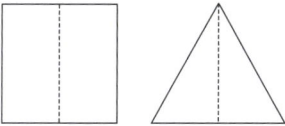

Now colour one half of each shape.

What do you notice?
Is one half the same on each shape?

💬 I notice that …

What is the same and what is different?

How did you find these questions? 🙂 😐 🙁

99

Fractions

Date:

Let's practise

1 Tick the cake that is cut in quarters.

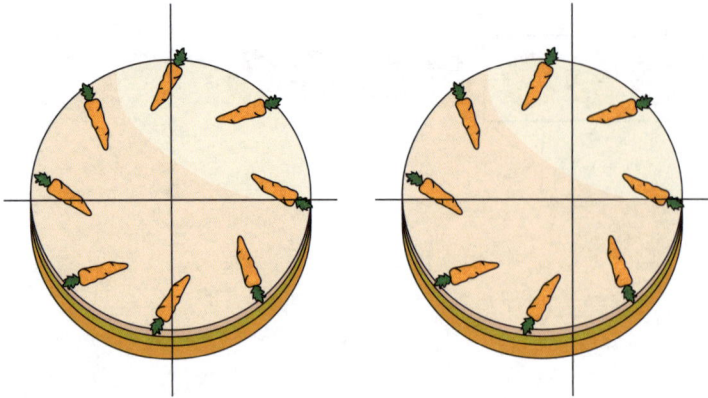

Remember, each quarter needs to be the same size!

2 Colour one quarter of each shape.

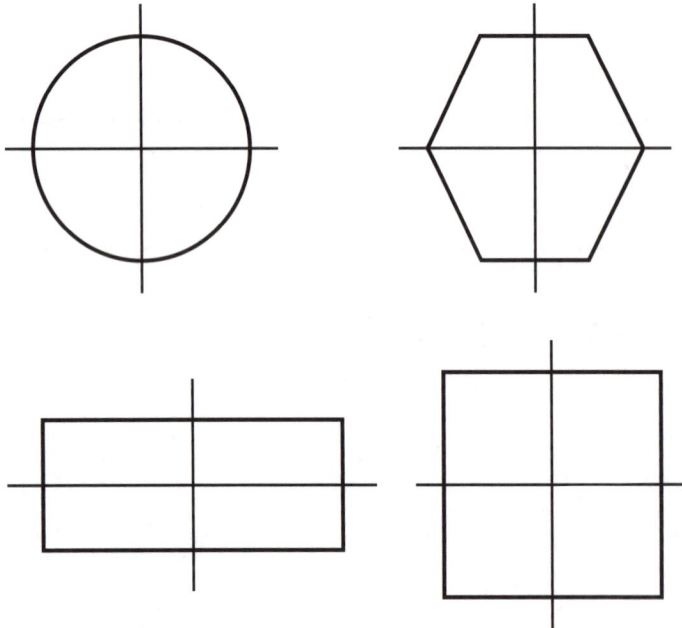

3 Draw lines to split the shapes in quarters.

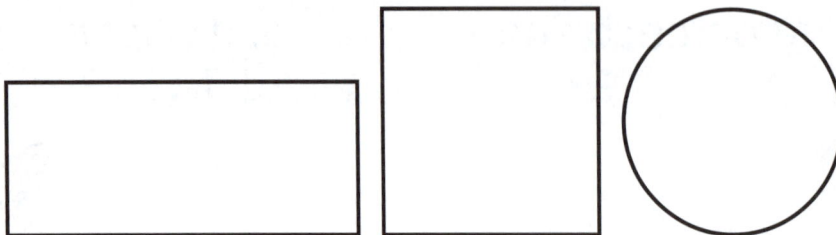

Remember to use a ruler!

4   Circle one quarter of each set of objects.

Then complete the sentences.

a)

One quarter of 20 is ☐

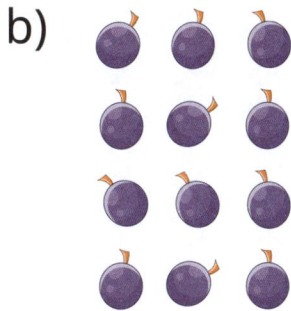

b)

One quarter of 12 is ☐

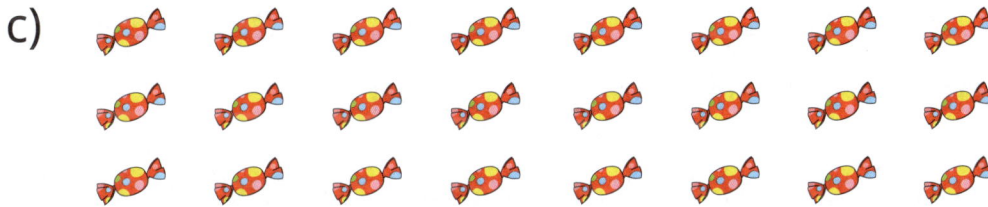

c)

One quarter of 24 is ☐

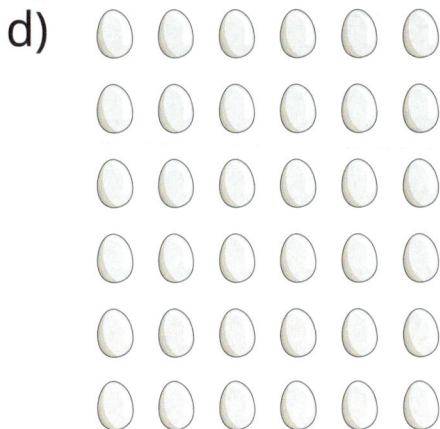

d)

One quarter of 36 is ☐

🏠 Real world maths

Use some objects around your home to find one quarter of different amounts.

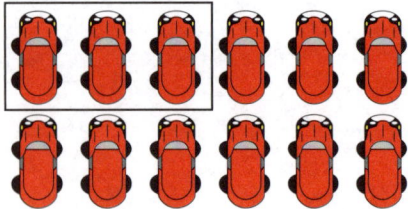

Talk it out

Cut some shapes out of pieces of paper.

Fold them in half and then in half again to make quarters.

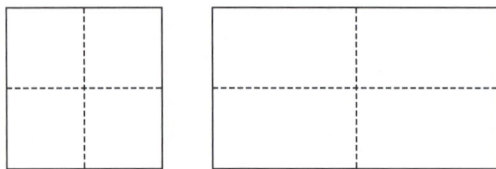

What is the same and what is different?

Now colour one quarter of each shape.

What do you notice?

Is one quarter the same on each shape?

I notice that ...

How did you find these questions? 🙂 😐 ☹️

Summer term

Block 3 Position and direction

In this block, we explore **position** and **direction**.

We use **left** and **right** to describe position.

The cat is to the left of the tree.
The dog is to the right of the tree.

We also describe position using **above** and **below**.

The apple is above the banana.

The apple is below the melon.

Here are some maths words that you'll see.

Can you remember what they mean?

position   direction   full/half/quarter turn   backwards

forwards   left   right   above   below

Position and direction

Date:

Let's practise

1   Match the turns to the descriptions.

quarter turn

half turn

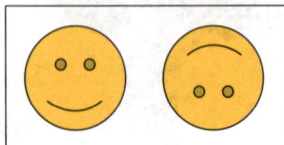

full turn

A **full turn** goes all the way round!

2   Here are some shapes.

Write [left] or [right] to complete the sentences.

a)   The square is to the _____ of the triangle.

b)   The rectangle is to the _____ of the circle.

c)   The circle is to the _____ of the square.

d)   The triangle is to the _____ of the circle.

3   Tiny is walking on a grid.

The arrow shows the way Tiny is facing.

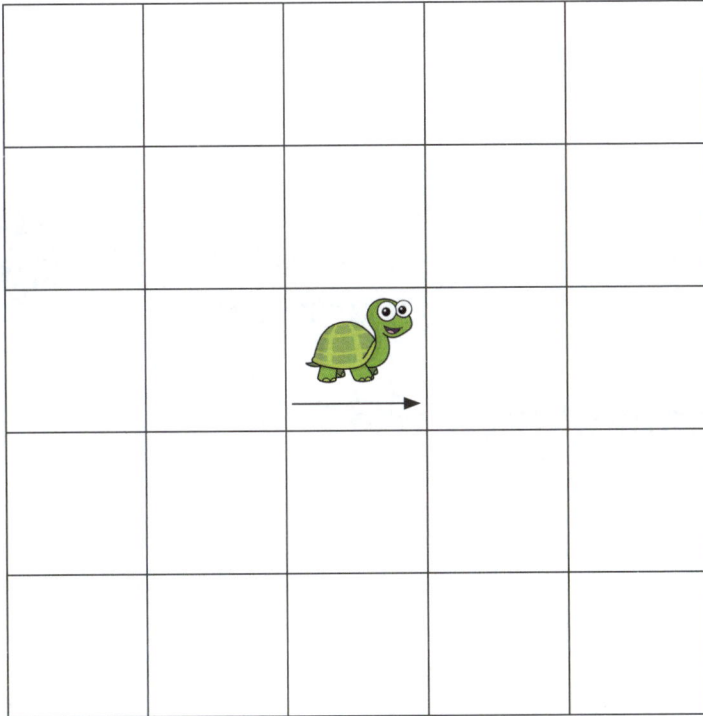

a)   If Tiny walks 1 square forward, draw a circle to show where Tiny will end up.

Which way is forwards and which way is backwards?

b)   If Tiny walks 2 squares backwards, draw a triangle to show where Tiny will end up.

4   Write above or below to complete the sentences.

a)   The beans are _____ the tube of crisps.

b)   The cereal is _____ the tube of crisps.

c)   The tube of crisps is _____ the cereal.

d)   The cereal is _____ the beans.

🧠 Think it out

Draw a picture to match the sentences.

- The square is above the circle.

- The star is below the circle.

- The rectangle is to the left of the circle.

Remember to check your left and right!

- The triangle is to the right of the circle.

💬 Talk it out

Go and stand in different places in your house and describe where you are.

You might be:

- behind the table

- to the left of the sofa

- below the light.

Depending on where you are facing, describe your position in different ways.

💬 I am standing …

💬 I am behind the …

💬 I am above the …

💬 I am to the right of the …
If I face the other way, I am to the left of the …

How did you find these questions?   🙂 😐 🙁

Summer term
Block 4 Place value

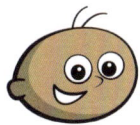

In this block, we **count** to 100

We use **base 10** to split numbers into **tens** and **ones**.

67 has 6 tens and 7 ones.

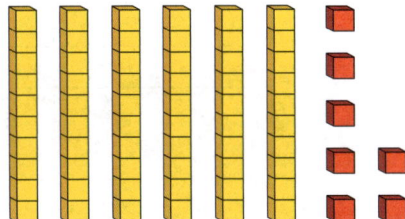

We use **number lines** to find **1 more** and **1 less** than a number.

73 is 1 more than 72

71 is 1 less than 72

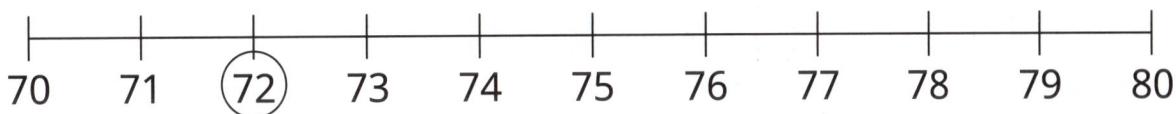

| 70 | 71 | (72) | 73 | 74 | 75 | 76 | 77 | 78 | 79 | 80 |

97 > 94

62 < 77

We **compare** numbers and write < and > to show **less than** and **greater than**.

97 is greater than 94

62 is less than 77

Here are some maths words that you'll see. Can you remember what they mean?

counting   tens   ones   1 more   1 less

compare   greater than   less than

Place value

Date:

Let's practise

1 Complete the number tracks.

a)

| 62 | 63 | 64 | | | | |

b)

| | | 75 | 76 | 77 | | | | |

c)

| | 90 | 89 | 88 | | | |

2 What numbers are shown?

a)

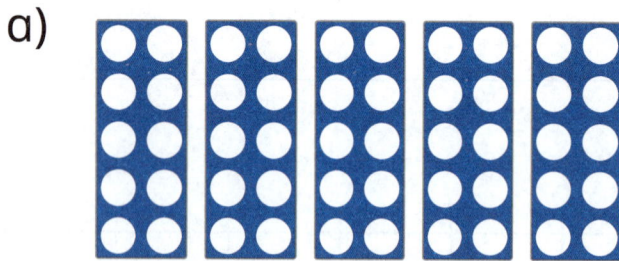

☐ tens = ☐

b)

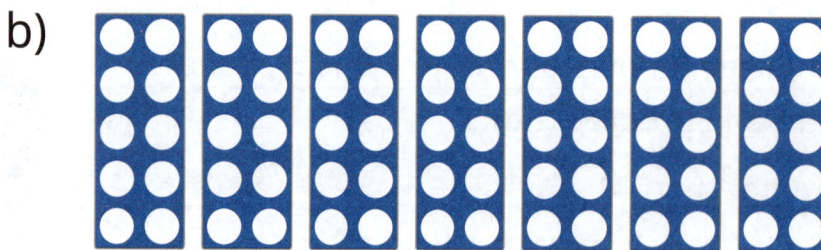

☐ tens = ☐

c)

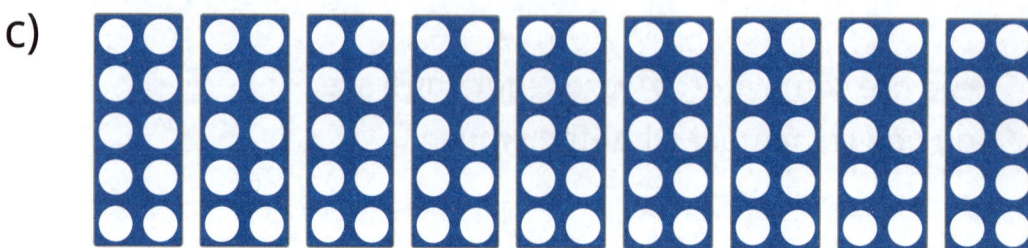

☐ tens = ☐

3 How many sweets are there? ☐

4 Use base 10 to complete the sentences.

a)

56 has ☐ tens and ☐ ones.

b)

92 has ☐ tens and ☐ ones.

> How many tens?
> How many ones?

c)

☐ has ☐ tens and ☐ ones.

5 Tiny is thinking of a number.

What number is Tiny thinking of? ☐

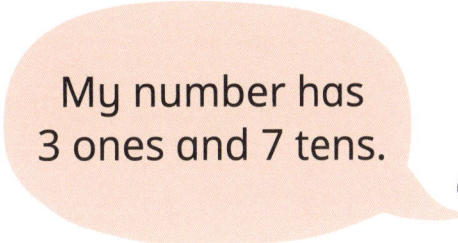

> My number has
> 3 ones and 7 tens.

🏠 Real world maths

Draw your own number track.

☐ ☐ ☐ ☐ ☐ ☐ ☐ ☐ ☐

Choose your first two numbers.

You can count forwards or backwards.

Ask someone at home to complete the number track.

Ask them to choose two different numbers to start
a new track.

Complete the number track.

Which two starting
numbers will you choose?

How did you find these questions?   🙂 😐 ☹️

Place value

Let's practise

1 Complete the number lines.

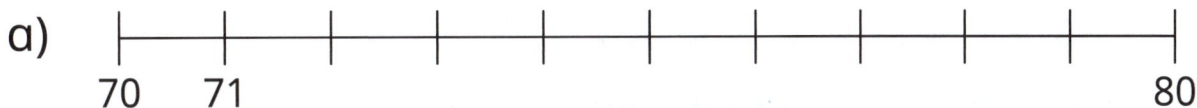

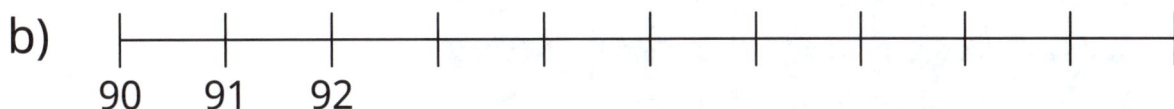

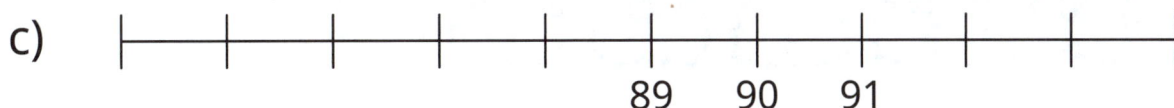

a)

```
├──┼──┼──┼──┼──┼──┼──┼──┼──┼──┤
70   71                                    80
```

b)

```
├──┼──┼──┼──┼──┼──┼──┼──┼──┼──┤
90   91   92
```

c)

```
├──┼──┼──┼──┼──┼──┼──┼──┼──┼──┤
                89    90    91
```

2 Here is a number line.

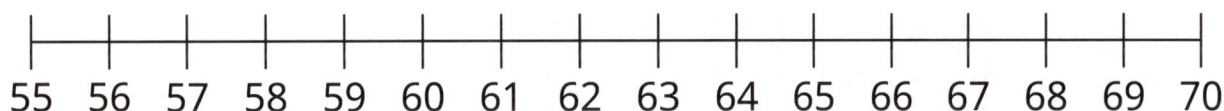

```
├──┼──┼──┼──┼──┼──┼──┼──┼──┼──┼──┼──┼──┼──┼──┤
55  56  57  58  59  60  61  62  63  64  65  66  67  68  69  70
```

a)   Circle 58

What number is 1 more than 58? ☐

What number is 1 less than 58? ☐

b)   Circle 64

What number is 1 more than 64? ☐

What number is 1 less than 64? ☐

c)   Circle 60

What number is 1 more than 60? ☐

What number is 1 less than 60? ☐

3   Circle the greater number.

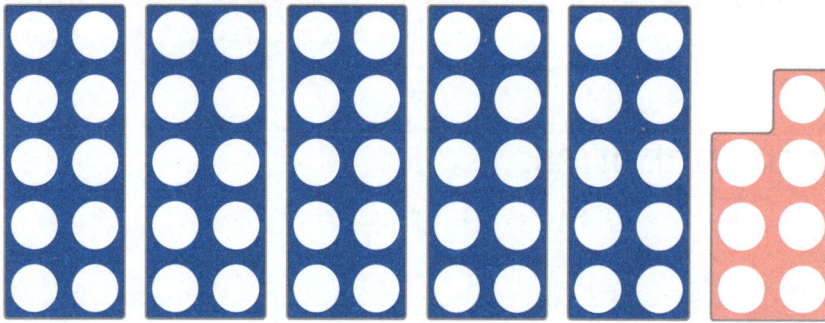

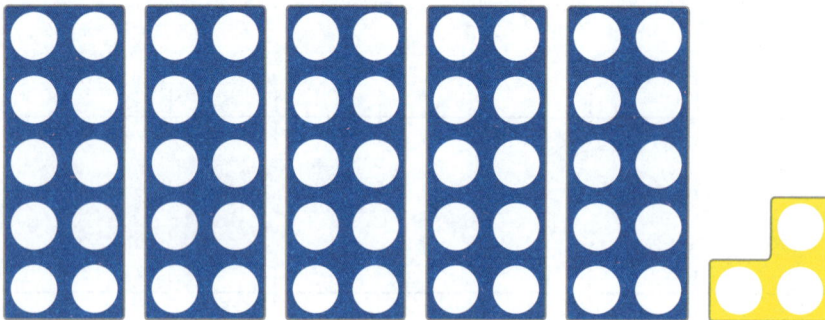

4   Circle the smaller number.

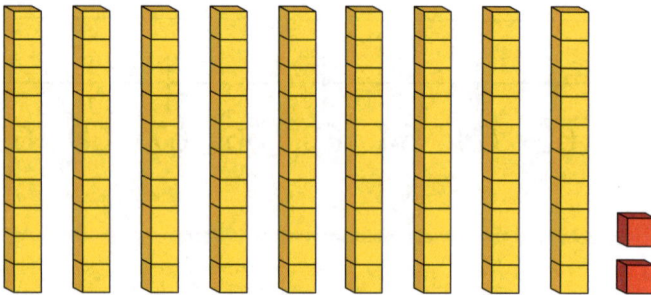

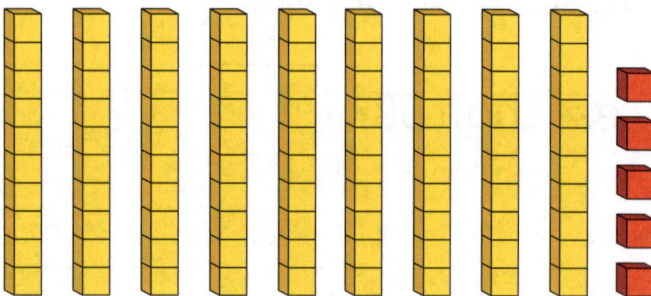

5   Write < or > to compare the numbers.

a)   82 ◯ 85   d)   67 ◯ 27

b)   99 ◯ 90   e)   53 ◯ 38

c)   29 ◯ 79   f)   100 ◯ 82

Remember, > means **greater than** and < means **less than**.

🏠 Real world maths

Make your own number line using string and paper.

| 70 | 71 | 72 | 73 | 74 | 75 | 76 | 77 | 78 | 79 | 80 |

Use your number line to find 1 more and 1 less than different numbers.

What do you notice?

_____

Which way is 1 more on the number line and which way is 1 less?

💭 Think it out

Ron and Kim are each thinking of a number.

1 less than my number is 89

My number has the same number of tens as Ron's number.

What number could Kim be thinking of? _____

Is there more than one possible answer?

How did you find these questions? 🙂 😐 🙁

Summer term
Block 5   Money

In this block, we explore **money**.

We find out about the value of different **coins** and **notes**.

Value	Coin
1 pence	1p
2 pence	2p
5 pence	5p
10 pence	10p
20 pence	20p
50 pence	50p
1 pound	£1
2 pounds	£2

Value	Note
5 pounds	£5
10 pounds	£10
20 pounds	£20
50 pounds	£50

We also use **number facts** to work out **how much** money there is.

I have 16 pence **in total**.

10p 2p 2p 2p

Here are some maths words that you'll see. Can you remember what they mean?

pounds   pence   total amount   how much   coins   notes

Money

Let's practise

1   What is the value of each card?

a) 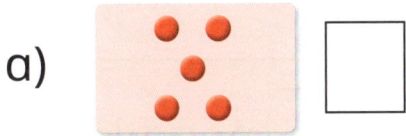 ☐

c) 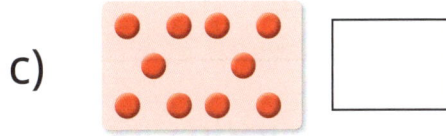 ☐

b)  ☐

d)  ☐

2   What is the value of each coin?

a)

☐ pence

c) 10p

☐ pence

> **Value** means how much something is worth.
>

b)  1p

☐ pence

d) 2p

☐ pence

3   How much money is there?

a)  2p 2p 2p 2p

☐ pence

> Which number facts can help you?
>

b)  5p 5p 5p 5p 5p 5p

☐ pence

c)  10p 10p 10p 10p 10p 10p 10p 10p

☐ pence

4 What is the value of each note?

a)

☐ pounds

c)

☐ pounds

b)

☐ pounds

d)

☐ pounds

5 How much money is there?

a)

☐ pounds

b)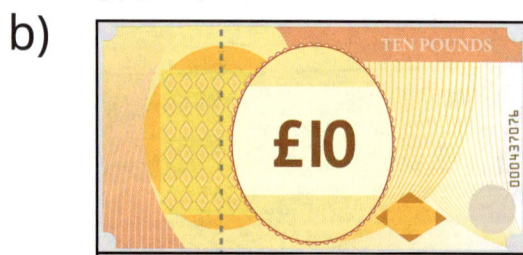

☐ pounds

6 Jack has some coins.

What coins does Jack have? _____

I have 12 of the same coin. I have 24 pence in total.

🏠 Real world maths

Find some coins around your home, or make some out of paper or card.

£1   £2   1p   2p   5p   10p   20p   50p

Sort them. How many of each coin do you have?

Type of coin	Number of coins	Total amount
1p		
2p		
5p		

Count the money.

How many 1p coins do you have? How many 2p coins? How will you count them?

I have _____ in total.

How did you find these questions?   😊   😐   🙁

Summer term
Block 6   Time

In this block, we look at **time**.

We explore the **days of the week**.

We look at the **months of the year** on a **calendar**.

My birthday is in June! When is yours?

Monday
Tuesday
Wednesday
Thursday
Friday
Saturday
Sunday

January	February	March	April	May	June
July	August	September	October	November	December

We also **tell the time**.

The first clock shows 3 **o'clock**.
The second clock shows **half past** 9

Here are some maths words that you'll see.

Can you remember what they mean?

day   week   month   year   second   minute   hour

o'clock   half past   before   after

Time

Let's practise

1   Tick what you do **before** eating.

wash up

wash hands

2   Tick what you might do **after** school.

watch TV

eat breakfast

3   Write all the days of the week.

Sunday, Monday, _____,

Wednesday, _____,

_____, Saturday

Try saying the days of the week out loud.

4   Write two things you do before you go to sleep.

_____

119

5 Complete the sentences.

a) The day **after** Tuesday is _____.

b) The day **before** Sunday is _____.

c) The day **after** Sunday is _____.

6 Here is part of a calendar.

| November 2023 | | | | | | |
S	M	T	W	T	F	S
			1	2	3	4
5	6	7	8	9	10	11
12	13	14	15	16	17	18
19	20	21	22	23	24	25
26	27	28	29	30		

A **calendar** shows the days and weeks in a month.

a) What month is shown? _____

b) On what date are the fireworks?

_____

c) What day is 10 November? _____

7 2 days after my birthday it is Saturday.

On what day is Jack's birthday?

_____

 Think it out

Max

My birthday is
in the month
before August.

My birthday is
in the month
after May.

Kim

Whose birthday is earlier in the year?

_____

> Max's birthday is in …
> I know this because …

> … comes before/
> after …

> Kim's birthday is in …
> I know this because …

🏠 Real world maths

Find a calendar at home.

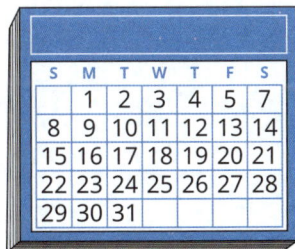

Choose another month.
What is the same and
what is different?

Choose a month.

What can you tell about that month by looking at the
calendar? _____

How many days are in the month? _____

What date is it on the first Monday of the month? _____

How did you find these questions?   🙂 😐 🙁

121

Time

Date:

Let's practise

1 Would you time these things in hours , minutes
   or seconds ?

a) Time it takes to eat a meal _____

b) Time is takes to do your homework _____

c) Time it takes to jump twice _____

d) Time it takes to paint a house _____

2 What time is shown on each clock?

a)

□ o'clock

c)

□ o'clock

b)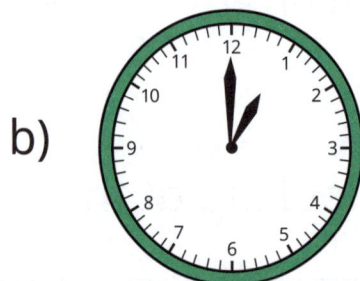

□ o'clock

d)

□ o'clock

3   What time is shown on each clock?

a)

Half past [ ]

c)

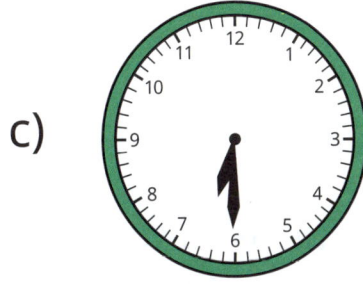

Half past [ ]

b)

Half past [ ]

d)

Half past [ ]

4   Draw the times on the clocks.

a)   7 o'clock

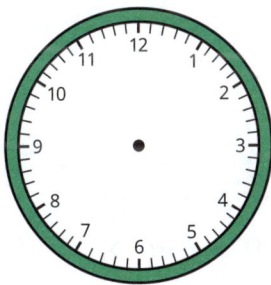

b)   Half past 11

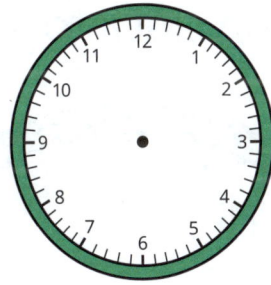

5   Tiny is telling the time.

It's 6 minutes past 5

Explain the mistake Tiny has made.

_____

🏠 Real world maths

Use a stopwatch to time how long it takes you to do these activities.

Record the time taken in seconds.

Activity	Time taken (seconds)
Clap 10 times	
Blink 8 times	
Eat an apple	

Which activity took the longest time?
Which took the shortest time?

💭 Think it out

Draw on the clock to show the time Kim goes to bed.

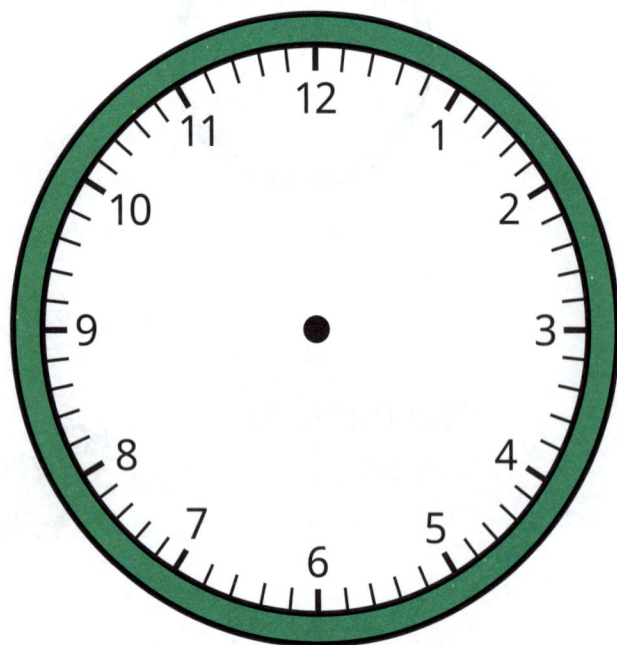

I go to bed
1 hour before
half past 8

How did you find these questions?   🙂 😐 🙁

Consolidation

Date:

Let's practise

1   7 tens subtract 7 ones = ☐

2

> The shape has been divided into quarters.

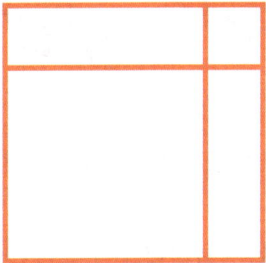

Do you agree with Tiny? _____

Explain your answer. _____

_____

3   Ron makes a number.

> My number is between 40 and 53

> The digits sum to 10

What number did Ron make?

☐

> Use number bonds to 10 to help!

4   Eva has 12 sweets.

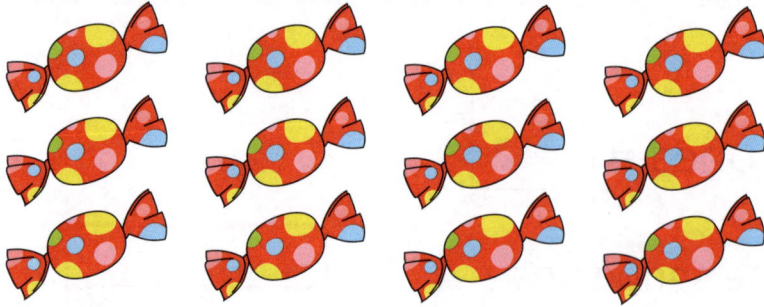

She gives Mo a quarter of the sweets.

She gives Teddy 5 sweets.

How many sweets does Eva have left?   ☐

5   Write <, > or = to make each statement correct.

$10 + 5 \bigcirc 10 - 5$

$6 + 2 \bigcirc 2 + 6$

$3 \times 10 \text{ pence} \bigcirc 3 \times 5 \text{ pence}$

6   Max has this money.

5p 5p 5p 5p

5p 5p 5p 5p

What is one quarter of Max's money?

☐ pence

🏠 Real world maths

Dora has this money.

(10p) (10p)

She spends one quarter of it.

How much does she have left? _____

Remember, there are 4 quarters in a whole.

🧠 Think it out

A packet contains 5 sweets.

Kim sells 4 packets on Monday.

She sells 3 more packets on Tuesday than she did on Monday.

How many sweets did she sell in total?

Count in 5s to help!

How did you find these questions?   🙂 😐 🙁

Time to reflect

Look back at the multiplication and division questions in Block 1.

Circle groups of 3 flowers.

How did you find it?

☺ I get it!   ☺ I need a little help.   ☹ I don't get it.

Look back at the halves and quarters in Block 2.

Draw a line to split the square in half. Draw lines to split the circle in quarters.

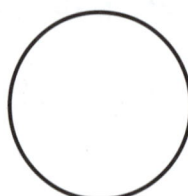

How did you find it?

☺ I get it!   ☺ I need a little help.   ☹ I don't get it.

Talk to someone at home about your work this term.
What went well? What do you want to practise?